Trifles from My Portfolio

Trifles from My Portfolio

The Adventures of a Young Medical Officer of
H.M. 66th Regt. in Portugal, Spain and India
1811-1817

Walter Henry

LEONAUR

Trifles from My Portfolio
The Adventures of a Young Medical Officer of H.M. 66th Regt.
in Portugal, Spain and India 1811-1817
by Walter Henry

First published under the title
Trifles from My Portfolio or Recollections of Scenes and Small Adventures
During Twenty-Nine Years' Military Service

Leonaur is an imprint of Oakpast Ltd

Copyright in this form © 2011 Oakpast Ltd

ISBN: 978-0-85706-651-0 (hardcover)
ISBN: 978-0-85706-652-7 (softcover)

http://www.leonaur.com

Publisher's Notes

The opinions of the authors represent a view of events in which he
was a participant related from his own perspective,
as such the text is relevant as an historical document.

The views expressed in this book are not necessarily
those of the publisher.

Contents

————retrorsiim
Vela dare atque iterare cuisus
————relictos.————

Horat.

To

SIR JAMES M'GRIGOR, BART., F. R. S.
DIRECTOR GENERAL OF THE ARMY MEDICAL DEPARTMENT,
THESE UNPRETENDING PAGES ARE INSCRIBED,
AS A STARK OF PERSONAL AND PROFESSIONAL RESPECT,
BY THE AUTHOR.

Preface

This little work is committed to a friendly public with some apprehension, but not without the hope of a reception more favourable than it deserves. The Author is conscious that he has exposed himself to a grave and just charge of presumption in the prominent obtrusion of his humble story on the community: still he cherishes some anticipations of forgiveness. Although it is acknowledged bad taste to make free with the first pronoun in our social intercourse, yet sometimes even egotism is overlooked when it is amusing, and we are apt to pardon a respectable *raconteur* who entertains the company with neat stories of personal adventure. Now, though this parallel may not quite hold good—for this supposition would be presumption upon presumption—the author fondly trusts, that if the reader should derive some small quantum of amusement from these "Trifles," he may have the good nature to extend the same indulgence to them as he would to the story-teller; notwithstanding that the staple of the book is the auto-biography of an obscure individual, who makes but a very Lilliputian hero.

CHAPTER 1

Childhood

I will a round, unvarnished tale deliver.
Shakespeare

Other arguments may be more cogent and logical, but the "*argumentum ad absurdum*" is often the most natural and convenient method of demolishing a faulty theory, or opinion. Thus, to disprove the notion, that the elements sympathize with our little individual concerns, on this planet, and even honour the birth, or lament the death, of a great man, by a flourish or peal of the band of nature, as was long fondly believed, it is only necessary to state the fact, that when so utterly insignificant an atom of humanity as myself came into the world—

The front of Heaven was full of fiery shapes
Of burning cressets———

the atmosphere growled its

———fierce and far delight,

as loudly as it did when Oliver Cromwell and Napoleon Buonaparte yielded up the ghost. For, I have been credibly informed, that on the early morning of the 1st of January, 1791, when the new year and myself were born together, there was a very terrible and uncommon accompaniment of rain, and tempest, and thunder, and lightning.

The moral world was, also, at that time, undergoing a storm far more dreadful, and of longer continuance, than the natural. Society was universally agitated, and more or less involved in the turmoil of the recent French Revolution, and all Europe was shaking still in this political earthquake. New elements in physics, as well as new theories in politics and ethics, were discovered and brought into play. A host of philosophers were starting up every week, each promulgating some new and startling hypothesis, and knocking down previous systems like ninepins. Paris was big with ominous and bloody events, and drawing near the parturition, whilst her sophists were preparing mankind for the monstrosities of the birth. The Abbé Sieyes was filling his desk with constitutions for nations of all ages and dimensions. Mirabeau was building up his tremendous reputation at the Jacobin Club. The emigrants were beginning their groans,—the Marseillois their hymns, and the Poissardes furies their yells.

Maximilian Robespierre was employed from morning to night in sharpening his dagger. Numerous aeronauts were fearlessly traversing the air in balloons; whilst Black, and Priestley, and Lavoisier, were taking it to pieces in their laboratories. In England, Pitt was employed in keeping down, with a strong hand, the surging sympathy of the mob with the lawless proceedings on the other side of the channel; or fighting nightly duels with his great rival in the House of Commons, or in manufacturing colonial constitutions, and making and fencing the warmest and most comfortable nests for political rattlesnakes in Lower Canada, Austria, and Russia, and Prussia, were engaged in those fearful Polish atrocities, which have since so palpably brought down on their heads, the vengeance of retributive justice. In short, all Europe was torn by the conflict of opposite opinions, interests, passions and prejudices; and in a state of universal hubbub, agitation, oscillation, perturbation, conglomeration, botheration and confusion.

Far removed from the chief scenes of all this strife, a little un-plumed biped, myself, first saw the light in the secluded and pretty little town of Donegal, in the north-west of Ireland, it is not necessary, my dear reader, to tell you more concerning my lineage, than, that it was respectable; and as to my ancestors, they were, at any rate, as numerous as those of the first duke in the land.

My native town is pleasantly situated on a small, but clear and pretty river, the Esk, where it meets the tide. It is no trifling advantage in after life to have been in possession of opportunities of acquiring habits of confidence in the water and powers of skilful swimming in early youth. Independent of considerations respecting the possible preservation of our own life, it is no small luxury to be able to save that of others.

Yet, my first acquaintance with the water was not a little unpropitious. When about four years old, I was taken out by a maid servant, one fine evening in summer, for a walk. She, of course, was enjoined to take particular care of Master Walter and not let him run into the wet places, for various reasons known to the learned; amongst the rest, for fear of spoiling his nice frock and trowsers. Above all things, she was ordered not to let him go out of her sight. The amiable sisterhood to which she belonged are remarkable for the punctuality with which they always follow such instructions. Now, there chanced to be a pleasant green lane near the town, much frequented for purposes of rural courtship, and to this favourite spot Dolly forthwith directed her steps, in the hope of enjoying a small palaver with a young baker of her acquaintance, who made his appearance, punctually, according to appointment.

Close to the place of meeting there happened to be a gate leading into a clean, flowery field, spangled with daisies and primroses, and clear of cattle. Into this field I was permitted to go for a hunt after the butterflies, whilst nurse and her lover remained in the lane. One side of my play ground was bounded by the river, which ran past its flowery bank in rather a swift current. Soon getting tired of the fruitless chase after the butterflies I sat down on this bank, and began to pull the bunches of primroses with which it was covered; but, unfortunately, in reaching for one tempting and luxurious bunch, near the water's edge, I lost my balance and tumbled in.

All hail, Frugality! Queen of the minor virtues and household decencies,—all hail! Thou carefully presidest over the minute concerns of our hearths and arrangest them into an aggregate of neatness, cleanliness and comfort. Thou sewest a button on the shirt collar of the cottager where an unseemly rent gaped before; nor dost thou scorn the more humble office of darning his Sunday hosen. Thou didst, perchance, condescend to pick up the very gray goose quill with which I write this small, but sincere tribute to thine excellent qualities, from the bleak common, where it lay desolate; and even the glossy and beautiful substance over which it now runs was once a worthless rag, until discovered by thy keen eye, and transmuted by thy wonder-working finger. Once more, then, all hail! for to thee I owe my life!

But, to descend from our heroics,—an article of considerable domestic importance, yclept starch, had lately been the subject of a little friendly controversy in our culinary circle. A new invention had been recently broached, and the national root had been taxed to furnish a species of starch, which brought with it, strong recommendations. The potato-starch was far cheaper, and was said to make clothes stiffer and whiter than the wheaten starch. The patriots of the day cried it up boisterously as a national production, to be patronized by all true-hearted Irishmen, and preferred to the Sassenach starch; and I am not quite sure that Mr. Daniel O'Connell, the great agitator, liberator, botherator and beggarman, did not make his debut in politics, by writing his first letter to the Irish people in its favour, from Douay, where he was then at college.

Be this as it may, my good father neither admired the new compound nor its credentials; for he was a genuine conservative of the orthodox *gluten*,—but it was a matter for female arrangement,—the womankind prevailed, and the potato-starch was procured. In the first trial of its strength, it fortunately chanced that my little white trowsers were super-saturated; and the consequent induration of my nether integuments, which had impeded my movements not a little, in the butterfly-hunt, furnished each tiny thigh with an air life-buoy in the water.

After floating down the current a few yards, just as my trowsers were beginning to melt, I providentially grounded on a shelving sand, and there I lay struggling and squalling. Although it could not be said that, like Don Juan on the beach, I was

As fair a thing as e'er was formed of clay,

for I was never superfluously handsome, yet I soon found, in my utmost need, a pitying Haidéé in the more homely shape of Dolly, my nurse.

As soon as she had finished her conversation with her lover, lengthened out, as usual, with many last words, Dolly began to think it was time to look after her charge; but he was nowhere to be seen. She explored the field unsuccessfully, till, on approaching the river, she, at length, caught a glimpse of poor Master Walter floating down the stream. Dolly, then, screamed with all her might, but the baker was out of hearing and there was no creature near, except an old goat, brousing on a bank. She ran down along the edge of the water, frightened out of her wits, and when the stream admitted of wading, rushed in desperately up to her middle, floundered to the shallow where I lay sticking in the mud, and dragged me to the shore.

The precise fib she invented, to account for my melancholy condition, when we came home, is not on record.

Dear reader, if my style should ever become turgid, or stifle, recollect how much I owe to starch.

The River Esk, (a common Celtic name for rivers in the British Islands,) after a short course of four miles from its parent lake amongst the mountains, enters the great Bay of Donegal, a little below the town. On a steep bank above the bridge, the base of which is washed by the stream, stands a fine old castle of the early Tudor era, formerly belonging to the great Earl O'Neill, but now, with the greater part of the town, the property of the Earl of Arran. This building, being considered a rich specimen of the architecture of that period, is surrounded on three sides by a modern wall, and preserved as much as may be from farther decay. The northern side of the castle rises high and abrupt from the rocky bank of the river, and is very richly mantled with ivy.

The only inhabitants of the interior of the castle, in my boyhood, were two large owls, who lived there, I believe, upwards of twelve years. But this wise and worthy pair were unfortunate in their family, for none of their progeny ever reached owl-hood. Whether it was that the climate was unfavourable, or the parent owls did not fondle the owlets judiciously, or pecked them too roughly, or did not keep their nest warm enough, or brought them old mice, too tough for infantile mastication, I know not; but the fact was, that no chick lived to adult age, and the old owl and his wife were left without children, to snore away their time, for want of better employment, with such apoplectic fervour as used often to startle myself and other little boys passing near the north front of the castle.

Yet, although these two *denizens* had kept possession for so long a time of the penetralia of the edifice, the umbrageous and flourishing ivy on the outside harboured a legion of jackdaws and sparrows. It happened that on a fine clear morning in February, having been presented, by my father, with a new gun and accompaniments, the reward of some piece of good conduct which I forget, I determined to make war on these birds, and to distinguish my first feat in arms, by the slaughter of a whole hecatomb.

Having made a reconnoissance before breakfast, I ascertained that the enemy was in great force, though in a state of relaxed discipline, which boded an auspicious result from a sudden and bold attack. I determined, therefore, as soon as I should swallow down my porridge, to surprise their position.

Breakfast over, and powder-horn and shot-belt indued, I seized my gun and marched boldly to the attack. After creeping on my hands and knees, till within thirty yards of the foot of the castle wall, the rocky nature of the soil preventing more regular approaches, I halted and began to load. I know not whether it arose from inexperience, or nervousness, at the vicinity of the point of attack, or flurry from the unusual mode of progression, or haste, or a bad lock; but, alas, the melancholy fact is but too certain, whatever the cause, that instead of bringing down materials for half a dozen sparrow pies, I blew myself up!

I never could find data to calculate how high I had been projected. The powder-horn contained exactly a pound of treble strong Dartford. Its brass head was found, some days after, about a quarter of a mile off, but it could throw no more light on the subject.

My first recollection of this horrible business is dated from a tub of suds in our wash-house, into which I had been soused, to put me out. After swallowing more soap than was agreeable, both in decoction and infusion, the larger grains of powder were well sponged out of my eyes, nostrils, mouth, and throat, and I was put to bed. In five minutes my kind uncle, Dr. R., and my sweet cousin, his daughter, were at my bedside.

About a fortnight afterwards, when my eyes began to open, I called for a looking-glass. The following, as nearly as I can recollect, was the amount of casualties:—

First.—One mahogany-coloured patch, occupying my forehead, peeling off at the edges, but fast aground in the middle.

Item.—Two eyebrows missing; supposed to have been shot into the ivy.

Item.—Two pairs of eye-lashes, *ditto ditto ditto*.

Item.—Two bits of wadding at anchor on the point of my nose

Item.—Two burnt beefsteaks in place of cheeks.

Item.—My curls, glossy and luxuriant, sublimed, and wandering through the atmosphere as curl-clouds.

Item.—Both hands tender as the lobster and red as its claw.

When quite recovered I abjured the gun and learned to fish. In process of time I became a very successful angler, a fact which many a

————*finny darter with the glittering scales*

has had reason to know to his cost.

16

CHAPTER 2

Boyhood

Nescio quid meditans nugarum, sed totus in illis.

Horat.

I fear it is but a poor apology for the obtrusion of the details of an humble individual's boyhood, on the public, to say, that the story is agreeable to the narrator by the pleasing-associations it evokes. Yet, I believe, this is the best excuse I can make for some of my early chapters, if not for the whole concern. My trifling historiette has small pretensions; but, insignificant as it is, I must tell it my own way, and trust to the good nature of my readers to excuse much of its contents.

From my early years I was a studious and reading boy, and had, fortunately, access to two respectable libraries, besides the. more limited one at home. Reading, indeed, was my greatest enjoyment, and I can still recollect the vivid delight with which I first perused the *Arabian Nights* and *Don Quixotte.* My young heart used to beat audibly for Shecherazade; and the catastrophe of the poor Don, abjuring his chivalry, burning his books, and dying penitent, made me melancholy for a week.

My parents were religious and taught me the Bible early; and, laughter-loving mortal that I am, I hope I have not forgotten their good lessons and that sacred instruction, assuredly the source and the spring of any humble merit I have ever possessed. Like uncle Toby, I was much struck with the military details, particularly the duel between David and Goliath, and the siege of Jericho. Even in my more mature judgment I admire the picturesque and most interesting account of this splendid beleaguerment exceedingly; the immense host of the Israelites moving seven days in solemn procession round the doomed city, preceded by the ark of the covenant and the sacerdotal trumpets; the solemn pause, on the seventh morning, only interrupted by the yet lingering echoes of the last blast charged with instant fate; the thunder-shout of an hundred thousand warriors, and the awful crash of the tumbling walls: then, the little graceful episode of the scarlet thread from the window, and the mercy to Rahab and her family. Verily, Uncle Toby, thou wert a man of taste. My own uncle was nearly as odd a personage as thou, and also a warm admirer of this magnificent siege.

But, (and I take some credit in telling it,) Joseph, delightful story of Joseph, to my early fancy, was full of the most absorbing fascination. How exquisitely simple and affecting, and how true to nature; how corroborative of the truth of the sacred page in which it stands. Well has it been observed by learned men, that nothing at all comparable to it, can be found in the whole range of sacred or profane history. Assuredly, the tale of Joseph will ever be as instructive and attractive as it has been and is; for it carries within it the unchangeableness of moral verity. There it remains, engraven in strong relief by the finger of the Almighty, admonishing to virtue and warning from crime!

The custom of reading in bed is bad and dangerous, yet such was the literary voracity with which I devoured any new book, that I often smuggled it to my couch and read as long as the candle lasted. Good Homer might take a nap over his *Illiad* if he chose, for nobody had a better right; but I can safely aver that I never did, either in the original, or Pope's or Cowper's translation. On the contrary, as good often springs from evil, my wakefulness over a book in bed, on one occasion, saved our family from destruction.

When the people of France chose to mix up a cup of blood for themselves and force it down each other's throats, they averred, lustily, that it was sweet and delicious to the taste, and very invigorating to the constitution. Under this specious character they palmed it on the neighbouring nations; and, amongst the rest, Ireland, deceived by the imposition, desired, greedily, to have a portion of the Circaean beverage, which she drank with mad heedlessness. She got drunk, and rose in rebellion, as a natural consequence. At the commencement of the rising the insurgents were much in need of arms, and, to procure them, used to pay nightly visits at houses where they supposed guns and pistols were to be found.

Now, my father's house was one of these; and on the identical night selected by the party, to pay their respects to our quiet family, I was busily engaged fighting with Cortes against the Mexicans, and fancying I heard the hideous sound from the gong of the idol temple rejoicing over a sacrificed Spaniard. Suddenly a real sound of men's feet in the garden, under my window, arrested my attention. It was between twelve and one, and all the house at rest; but I started up instantly and awoke the family. As those were ticklish times, firearms were always kept loaded; my father seized a blunderbuss, and two men servants a gun each.

A window was then cautiously opened, and a parley ensued; but, as the rebel party, apparently ten or twelve in number, insisted on all the arms in possession being given up incontinently, threatening death in case of refusal, and my father peremptorily declined the terms, the negotiations were soon concluded. The villains then prepared to force the back door, and one strong ruffian had already battered in two or three panels with a sledge-hammer, when a window above his head was suddenly opened, and my father shot him dead on the spot. Some desultory firing then took place; the gang uttered the most horrid threats of fire and extermination to all in the house; but, another of them being hit, they became alarmed, and, finally, decamped, carrying with them the dead body.

My uncle, the physician, was a man of letters and had a good library. Having lost his only son, who was surgeon of a man-of-war and died in the West Indies, and finding me docile and studious, he took a fancy to me, which, gradually, ripened into affection, and I found myself, in process of time, established in the vacuum in his heart, which the sad bereavement of his excellent son had left. One beloved daughter remained to console and bless her widowed parent. Her mother was dead.

Catharine R—— was three months younger than myself, and my playmate, friend and confident, from infancy. She was a pretty, graceful and clever girl, playful as a kitten, but of a very sweet and generous disposition. When I was so terribly scorched by the gunpowder she used to sit by my bedside with one of my own sisters, but to no one would she concede the task of applying the cooling lotions to my face, and reading amusing stories to assuage the smart. When able to move about, her smiling and ingenuous face was, generally, the first object I saw peering into the parlour after breakfast, when she paid her daily visit of kind enquiry and sympathy. She was very frequently permitted to be my companion on my short angling excursions, when the weather was fine; and then she would trip along the bank like a fairy, carolling her light song, making bouquets of wild flowers, picking berries, or chasing butterflies with her little silk-haired dog, Cato.

Even as I write, how vividly does not my retrospective glance embrace the accompaniments of one of these excursions, and my ear yet drink in the sweet accents of my cousin's voice. The colours seem fresh as yesterday; the lightly dappled sky; the spring of the lark from the meadow, and his instant gush of song from mid-heaven; the murmur of the quiet river, or the more noisy brawling of an eddy around some favourite rock, in shelter of which lay the trout I marked for my own; the small circle raised by some tiny fish on the placid surface, or the heavy plunge of a salmon; the cheerful note of Catharine in concert with the sweet twitter of the wren, or more ambitious song of the goldfinch, from the thicket, on the opposite bank. O, innocent and enchanting scenes of my youth, would that I could again enjoy you with the same pure and gushing freshness of heart as in days of yore!

Softly, softly, good sentimental Sir; perhaps, on reflection, it is better as it is. Could we relive our youth, we must, I suppose, take our memory back with us, and I fear, in that case, our boyish delights would appear somewhat insipid after the more exciting and tumultuous raptures of maturer years; the plaudits awaiting eloquence; the triumphs of ambition; successful love and glorious battle. Yes, it is better as it is; the freshness of youth and innocence would then, I fear, be only *eau sucré* after champagne.

It is therefore, better as it is; boys love boyish sports because they have never known an thing better. By a wise and beneficent ordination, every stage of life, like every season of the year, has its own peculiar enjoyments, and if the remark is not original, as few sentiments we utter can be—it is not the less true.

My cousin, who died in the West Indies, had caught and tamed a large gray seagull, which he called Simon. After the death of his amiable master this bird became a great favourite with my uncle and all the family, and used to run about the yard quite domesticated and on good terms with the poultry. He would answer to his name and come to be fed even more quickly than the rest; for a certain spice of early voracity still stuck to him, despite his civilization and breeding. If an unfortunate mouse was caught and thrown into the yard, the gull, from a quicker eye and former habits, would be sure to distance his competitors in a race for the prize, and gobble it up before any of them. One of his wings was kept clipped; but, notwithstanding, he generally managed to take up a position on one of the high pillars of the gate, from whence he could reconnoitre the poultry-yard and garden; being unwilling to forego altogether his serial explorations. From this circumstance, my humorous uncle called him, "Simon Stylites," who, as the learned reader knows, was an ancient Egyptian hermit that lived thirty years on the top of an obelisk.

There was a large fishpond in the garden which was fed by a small rivulet. After my cousin's death it was much neglected and became covered with weeds. At this time I had become a successful angler, and often contributed a salmon or some nice red trout for my uncle's table, he and his daughter being fond of fish. One day when we were all three walking in the garden, I proposed to have the pond cleared out, and promised to stock it with trout, which might be tamed and taught to come for crumbs from the hand of Catharine. The old gentleman embraced the suggestion and gave orders accordingly, whilst his fair daughter's eyes sparkled at the idea of feeding the finny pets.

When the pond was ready I took measures for catching a number of small trout and transmitting the little captives to their new abode; and in the course of a week I stocked it with some dozens. Three or four days after, my uncle went to inspect the condition of his new subjects, but was much surprised to find they had all disappeared. As his maxim was the indulgent English sentiment that supposes innocence without proof of guilt, no suspicion fell on Simon, who still marched about the yard among the turkeys with all imaginable gravity and propriety. I had my own private opinion on the subject, however, which was, by no means, favourable to Mr. Simon. In a few days a second batch of trout was procured, and, this time, a watch was set to discover the culprit. Alas, for honest appearances—my poor uncle had been *gull'd*, like cleverer people who trust implicitly to a grave face; for, the very next morning after the reservoir had been re-stocked, Simon Stylites was discovered in *flagrante delicto*, and slunk off as soon as I made my appearance, with all the consciousness of detected guilt, to herd among his poultry cronies.

There were various opinions as to the proper punishment to be awarded in the case. As to the offence being treated as a capital felony, it was altogether out of the question; for my uncle would rather fill up his fish-pond than suffer any thing to be done affecting the life of his son's favourite bird. At last, it struck me, that I might devise a plan to punish the offender for his gluttony, and cure him of the vice at the same time; which, according to the most enlightened jurisconsults, would be accomplishing the grand desiderata of criminal justice.

Next morning, before the fowl-house where Simon lived was

open, I fastened two small trout on unbarbed hooks and threw them into the fish-pond with lines attached to them; then, hiding myself behind a lilac on the bank, with the lines in my hand, I awaited the result. I had no occasion to wait long; for, at the same time as the day before, the sage-looking bird strutted down the gravel walk to the edge of the pond, and proceeded to reconnoitre with all due precision. Having soon discovered the decoy-fish, which were near the surface, down he darted on them, instanter, with all the rapacity of his early days, not a bit modified by his civilized education.

When I saw that he was fairly caught, I started up and pulled the lines, and soon had my friend Simon floundering about in a state of astonishment. After playing him as long as I considered proper, for the purposes of justice, I extricated the hooks from his mouth and liberated him with an admonition. Now, although advice in such cases is generally thrown away, and many an asthmatic Judge might save the valuable breath he thus idly wastes on emancipated criminals, this was, by no means, the case with my reprimand. On the contrary, it produced the most salutary effect on the morals of the seagull: the result would have delighted old Jeremy Bentham, could he have witnessed it; the fish flourished, and the reformed Simon Stylites never visited the forbidden precincts again during the rest of his life.

CHAPTER 3

Boyhood Continued

The valley rings with mirth and joy;
Among the hills the echoes play
A never, never ending song
To welcome in the May.
                    Wordsworth.

—————*but near the well*
That never fails, the golden pimpernel
Enjoys the freshness of this Alpine clime;
And violets linger in each deep cold dell,
As lovely virtues of the olden time
Cling to their cottage homes and slowly yield to crime.
                    Elliott.

All the world knows that Moliere always read his comedies to his old woman before producing them on the stage, and judged by the effect on her what he might expect from the audience. So, to compare great things with small, I never mounted a new fly without making it pass an ordeal, though not exactly of the same nature. As I had no old woman, and even if I had, her optics would scarcely answer, I was obliged to employ a venerable cat.

This tabby was somewhat particular in her tastes. She loved milk and fish as well as ordinary cats, and often regaled herself with a tender mouse when she could; but she differed from her race in being fond of flies. It is true she had no inclination for the larger kinds, and would turn up her nose at a bluebottle—still she relished the lighter and more delicate genera, and appeared to enjoy a small-bodied, long-leg'd, fly, such as a green or gray drake, as much as we would a snipe or a woodcock. When I found the light favourable, and grimalkin opening her eyes after a doze on the rug, I used to suspend the fly to be examined opposite a small crack in the window-pane in the full light of the sun. The slight current of air, through the crack, agitated it sufficiently to give it the appearance of life. If it was destined to be a killing fly, the old lady looked greedy, twirled her long moustaches and struck the rug three or four times with her tail. If otherwise, she took no notice, but resumed her nod. Under the sanction of her approval I proceeded to my sport with all the confidence of a Roman, to whom the Augur had promised victory.

The schoolboy is proverbially happy when sallying out on a fine holyday morning, gun or fishing-rod in hand, in all the exuberance of youthful spirits, and cheered and stimulated by the hope of success. I well remember with what buoyant gladness I hasted along the path, by the river-edge of the meadow that led up to the best fishing part of my native stream. As I said before, its course is short, but the valley through which it runs is pretty, and in some places almost beautiful, but the beauty is of the quiet order. The Esk, here, is such a stream as might be imagined watering a Lorraine landscape—sinuous, gliding, unpretending and translucent: no noise, save the murmur of a gentle current—no rapids—no cataracts—no nonsensical bursts of fluvial passion ending in froth and folly. A Naiad might safely invite a Dryad, from the neighbouring mountain, to breakfast; and both might sit thereafter in amicable colloquy, on the flowery bank, without a ripple on the placid stream big enough to wet their garters.

The valley of the Esk is studded with curious round hills of no great elevation, resembling inverted basins; which are all very well defined and regular. These hills have usually a fringe of ash, sycamore, white-thorn, and alder round the base, and are cultivated up the acclivities; with, for the most part, a good looking farmhouse at the top.

In my young days this vale was inhabited by a moral, industrious, hardy and good-looking population, who were, chiefly, Protestants. I have heard with concern that many of this estimable peasantry have, since then, emigrated to America and Australia.

In those days my memory was retentive, and I had Virgil, and Horace, and Milton, and Shakespeare, and most of the English Poets, at my finger-ends. Owing, probably, to early religious training, Cowper was an especial favourite, and I love him still; *cum grano salis.* I have often wondered why some sensible physician of his acquaintance did not attack his hypochondriac delusions through the liver and stomach—undoubtedly the *"fontes malorum."* And with every sincere respect for true religion, in the value of which I am a cordial believer, I have the presumption to be of opinion, that had I lived at Olney, my blue-pilling the poet would have done him far more good than all the heavy lectures his friend Newton so mercilessly showered upon him.

When Scott appeared I devoured each successive poem with the most hungry avidity, and considered them all great efforts of genius. Nine-tenths I now esteem namby-pamby. But the battle-piece in *Marmion*, and a few other portions, still maintain their ground.

During my angling peregrinations, it was my habit and pastime to recite aloud some favourite poem which I had lately read, in sauntering along the river's banks; thus, exercising voice and memory, and mingling a small portion of the "*utile*" with a large share of the "*dulci*." One beautiful morning in June, I thus strolled up the valley as high as the lake, purposing to return by the opposite bank of the stream. The day was delightful, the air balmy, and not too hot; being tempered by a gentle south-west wind, or that mild Favonian breeze, so grateful to the senses along the western shores of Europe, and so dear to anglers. The sky was hung with festoons of white fleecy clouds, the shadows of which would darken the water, momentarily, and disguise, nicely, the artificial appendages of the fly, and then glide across the valley and ascend the uplands. The bushes were musical; the trees in the first freshness of their verdant honours; and the whole face of nature was covered with one radiant smile.

At this time, I was yet only a trout-fisher and innocent of salmocide. But I felt that morning such an exuberance of "lusty life" and high spirits as could only be presages of my approaching good fortune. When I reached a favourite place where I had frequently caught some fine trout, I heard a sudden splash in the water, and, on looking a little down the stream, there, without doubt, were the large expanding circles on the surface, caused by the rise of a salmon. I had only a small rod and slender silk line, but they were good of their kind, and I determined to dare the contest.

Approaching the place, then, with some such feeling as the harpooner experiences when poising his weapon for a plunge into a whale, or the matador when preparing to give the *coup de grâce* to a bull, I threw my flies lightly over the spot where the fish had risen, whilst my heart palpitated violently and my whole frame trembled with excitement. Up he darted at the fly, but I struck too soon and missed him, and a second time I was equally unsuccessful. After giving him a little leisure to compose himself, I again placed the tempting object within his reach, and once more he dashed at it, but carelessly and contemptuously, as if he purposed, by a stroke of his tail, to wet the nimble wings that had eluded him before. This last and lucky time, I hooked the fish, but by the edge of the tail—a most untoward place; for, thus hooked, every fish has tenfold advantages and chances of escape.

When I found the salmon fast on the line, I felt something akin to the sensation of being in the clutch of a tiger. *Whiz, whiz, whiz*, sounded the reel—away, away, away, darted the fish, like John Gilpin, or Mazeppa. Fortunately, the bank of the river was the edge of an extensive meadow, clear of trees, so that when my line was run out I could run too. As the chase proceeded and Mr. Salmo began to feel a little tired with pulling me after him, I gained on him perceptibly, and began to wind up. Once more, he would be off like a shot, with a leap in the air, when he halted, five or six feet high, shewing me distinctly all his fair proportions. He made about a score of these summersaults, whilst the whirr of his fins and tail in the rarer element was like the rising of a covey of partridges. After an arduous struggle of two hours, I fairly tired him out, and landed him on a shelving bank. He was a fine fish of twelve pounds, fresh from the sea; and as I stood over him in triumph, where he lay gasping on the sward, the feeling was only comparable to the exultation of Achilles bestriding the corpse of Hector.

That day I fished no more; but hurried home to exhibit the "*spolium opimum*," and lay my prize at my fair cousin's feet.

There was a mill on the Esk, about a mile from my native town, the neighbourhood of which used to be capital fishing ground. A portion of the stream had been turned off the main body and made the feeder of the mill-dam; this, after a flood, and whilst it yet retained a rich brown tint, so dear to the fishing fraternity, was, generally, full of the lake trout, and furnished me many an hour's amusement. But, as there is nothing mundane without alloy, there was one small drawback. The miller's ducks and geese, considering that they had a right to use the water-privileges in their own territories, were always in my way—swimming and splashing about in the mill-course and frightening away the trout. Provoked with their spoiling sport, I used sometimes to throw my flies amongst them and hook one of them by the foot. The frightened bird would attempt to fly away, but, after allowing it a little play, I would catch it, take out the hook and let it off.

This was all very well when no champion for the feathered people was in sight; but I had a certain latent and unpleasant apprehension of evil from the miller's wife—a cross and masculine lady, the terror of all the little boys in the neighbourhood—who would be likely to punish on my ears the indignities sustained by her ducks. One day, whilst in the very act of amusing myself with one of the poultry, I descried this formidable dame with a child in her arms, on the other side of the mill-stream. The quacking of the bird soon attracted her attention, and, "sending her voice before her"—in a volley of curses, like one of the Homeric heroes, she ran to a plank that crossed the stream, with the too evident intention of passing to my side and taking certain liberties with my person. As it would have been very unmilitary to permit this hostile movement without interruption, I straightway threw down my rod, and ran to defend the *tête du pont* on my own bank; and when I found she was storming the pass and already half-way across, I pushed aside a prop on which the plank rested; when the enemy lost her footing and was tilted into the water.

In an instant I felt the most bitter compunction and that intolerable consciousness of deserving to be hanged. The mother managed to scramble to the bank, but, in her fright she lost hold of the poor infant, which was hurried down by the current straight towards the sluice that opened on the mill-wheel. Being resolute to repair the mischief I had done, I jumped in, and in a few strokes reached the unconscious little creature just as it was entering the immediate suction of the sluice. I seized it, swam to the shore and then delivered it to the mother, with a full confession of guilt, entreaty for pardon and promise of amendment.

By this time the miller, attracted by his wife's screams, made his appearance, and I prepared for a very comfortable drubbing—if not something worse. But after the first burst of passion I was most agreeably disappointed, for they both behaved with great magnanimity. I pleaded my own cause as well as I could; and as the place where the plank crossed the stream was not deep, an absolutely felonious *malus animus* could not be established. Evidence as to good character and respectable family, too, was not wanting; and the promptitude with which I had rescued the poor child was in my favour. Finally, I was forgiven, and a treaty of peace was established, in which the interests of the ducks and geese were guaranteed for the future. When all this was happily completed, I was invited to dry my clothes at the kitchen fire, before which half a dozen oaten-cakes were standing. One of these was presented to me as a peace-offering—the infant was undressed, dried, and soon soothed to sleep; and a little silver rattle from the town, the next day, won the mother's entire forgiveness.

One Saturday, Catharine and Cato got leave to accompany me. We followed the bank of the river, along the meadow, to a famed haunt of trout, called the "Common Hole," where a small river joins the main stream. Many a speckled beauty have I tossed on the green sward out of that hole in days of yore. When we reached the confluence of the rivers, I put my tackle in order, and was soon going on prosperously and fast filling my pannier—Catharine, in the meanwhile, being busily occupied in manufacturing wild-flower nosegays, or hunting the brilliant June butterflies over the field, assisted by little Cato, who appeared to relish the sport as much as his mistress.

I had now hooked a large trout and was playing it with great care, altogether absorbed by my sport; when I heard a loud scream of terror, and on looking up I was horrified to behold poor Kate running towards me without her bonnet, exclaiming, "O, Walter—the bull—the bull!" whilst a furious black brute was pursuing her, at the distance of a couple of hundred yards, tearing up the earth with his horns and bellowing frightfully. There was, evidently, not a moment to lose; but, what to do, I knew not. With desperate energy I seized the fishing-rod, and after directing my cousin to run for her life to the gate of the field, I advanced as boldly as a palpitating heart would permit, to meet the bull. It was, indeed, a forlorn hope—still, I cherished the idea, that the human voice has a magic power of subduing the fiercest animal, which I had recently picked up in the course of my reading; accordingly, I strained my voice to the loudest shout possible, and ran menacingly at the fierce beast, brandishing my fishing-rod.

Whether his ear was annoyed at the shrillness of my treble, or his eye magnified the long rod into a formidable weapon, I know not; but he stopped, when within ten yards of me, glaring on me and tossing off the sward in fragments from his horns. As soon as he had ascertained the real insignificance of his foe, he began to bellow afresh, lowering his head for a last rush, and I gave myself up for lost. As I was turning towards the hole where I had been so peacefully enjoying myself five minutes before, with the intention of making a run and a plunge into the water, all at once, my dear little ally, Cato, came into play. With the magnanimity of his Roman namesake, he had scorned to abandon a friend in distress, and instead of flying with his mistress, had remained with me, at the post of danger. The courageous little animal now ran up within a few feet of the bull's horns, barking as fiercely as he could and making an important diversion in my favour.

As soon as I saw the beast's attention momentarily occupied by his puny antagonist, I took to my heels and arrived at the gate in time to assist my poor panting Kate, who had scarcely strength or breath left to climb over. Presently, up came the bull roaring, in pursuit of Cato; but, like many other runaways, I shewed a firm face in my intrenchments; and having plenty of ammunition at hand, in the form of a heap of broken stone for mending the road, I opened a sharp fire on the enemy's forehead through the bars of the gate, and, after one effective shot in the eye, succeeded in beating him off.

Although both much frightened, we soon recovered; the glory of the close of the engagement cheering us up mightily, avid determined not to lose our day's amusement, nor leave the spoils of battle as trophies in the possession of the enemy. Accordingly, when we saw the bull retiring, I followed at a very respectful distance—secured my cousin's bonnet and parasol, and my own rod and basket, and we proceeded farther up the river, where I succeeded in filling the pannier; and, notwithstanding the threatening aspect of affairs in the morning, we returned home in high spirits.

Chapter 4

Boyhood Conclusion

—————Such
The Esk o'erhung with woods, —————
—————*Hail! sacred flood.*
May still thy hospitable swains be blest
In rural innocence; thy mountains still
Teem with thy fleecy race; thy tuneful woods
For ever flourish; and thy vales look gay
With painted meadows and the golden grain.
Armstrong.

In the course of my boyish explorations of the banks of my native river, I have seen and known a great deal respecting the habits and natural history of the salmon and the cognate trout races, and become acquainted with some curious particulars, a short relation of which may not be uninteresting.

The physical structure of fishes, so beautifully adapted to the nature of the element in which they live and move, has been the subject of especial notice and admiration amongst philosophers from the earliest times. But, though the wedge-shaped head—the gradual enlargement of the body—the beautiful machinery of the fins—the mailed skin—the ballasting air-bladder and the rudder-tail, demonstrate the divine and transcendent wisdom with which they were formed for swift and easy progression in the water, the use of the brilliant colouring with which the skins of many *genera* are adorned is not so manifest; and would almost appear a waste of bright tints, lavished amidst the dim twilight of the deep. Yet, from all analogy, we may be well assured that this is not without an object; and farther, that it may even serve purposes of the greatest importance in the economy of nature.

The tiny lump of the glow-worm and firefly, so delicately beautiful, is the beacon for the male insect. Thus, the gorgeousness of the skins of fishes may be necessary to guide and keep together the different families in their devious wanderings through the vast spaces they traverse. Be this as it may, the painted skin of the fish, considered merely as ornamental, harmonizes in the creation with the rich fur of the quadruped—the brilliant plumage of the bird—the blossoming glory of the tree—and, above all, the exquisite adornment of the flower. Though we may never know fully the objects and uses for which this splendid profusion was bestowed, all should be reverentially viewed as the boon of measureless goodness and beneficence. We can conceive that a dull monotonous uniformity of shape, and sombre colours, might have characterized the animal and vegetable kingdoms; but it has pleased the Deity to fill the heavens and the earth, and even the waters under the earth, with diversified beauty, and to confer only on his rational creature, man, the capacity to comprehend and enjoy it.

Conspicuous amongst the finny tribes, as well for the quality of the delicious flesh, as for great symmetry of form and elegance of colouring, are the *salmonidae* or salmon-family—but, principally, the *salmo salar*, or common salmon, appropriately placed, by Cuvier, at their head. In fact, we can scarcely conceive anything more perfect than the physical and moral character (if I may so use the word) of this noble fish. He is moulded in accordance with our notions of great muscular strength, combined with lightness of outline; and every quality of the animal corresponds with his appearance. His tunic of rich silver tissue is in the chastest taste—"*simplex munditiis*"—his movements in his own element are peculiarly easy and graceful; he is fastidious in his food, as a fish of such high blood ought to be; but he can, on emergency, bear hunger well, and even total abstinence, for weeks, without injury. His spirit is ardent, adventurous and persevering, and his speed is great.

Most intelligent persons are aware that our favourite fish is a great and intrepid traveller, migrating annually from the sea to the fresh water, and ascending the largest rivers to their distant sources. Influenced by unerring instinct, it quits the sea in spring or early summer; waits, generally, for a flood in the stream it purposes to visit, and then dashes on, at a rate inversely proportioned to the rapidity of the current and nature of the obstacles it meets with, until it reaches its destination in the upper and shallow waters; where it may look out for a mate, and take measures for the important business of propagating its kind.

When a strong rapid, or even a fall of ten or twelve feet occurs, the salmon surmounts the impediment with little difficulty; but when the stream is deep and full, and the fall considerable, the poor fish is obliged to stop, and appears sadly puzzled. He soon reconnoitres, in all directions, for a passage, and even leaps out of the water, apparently with no other object than to get a peep from a higher position; though, I confess, that the structure of his eye is rather against this supposition.

Salmon-leaps are objects of great curiosity and interest. There are many in Europe—particularly in Norway and the British Islands—two of the most remarkable of the latter are at Ballyshannon and Coleraine, in the North of Ireland—with the former of which I am well acquainted, being only ten miles distant from Donegal.

The large and beautiful lake, Loch Erne, fifty miles long by ten or twelve broad, pours its waters into the Atlantic by a short and very rapid river, which, after an impetuous course from Belleek, and a last fall of fifteen or sixteen feet at Ballyshannon, meets the tide at the bottom of a perpendicular limestone rock. The open sea is only three miles distant from the fall; and in early summer innumerable salmon run up the river and assemble in "the pool," as the abyss below the rock is called, checked in their career by this formidable barrier. In the course of a week many thousands are here collected, waiting, as it would almost appear, for a spring-tide to raise the water in "the pool" and make the leap easier. Here, the fish are taken in nets, in great numbers, and generally sent to London.

Men, however, are not here the only fishers. Seals follow the fish from the sea and prey upon them in "the pool," pursuing them with greater speed and success than the unwieldy appearance of these amphibious creatures would lead one to expect. They are often seen emerging from the froth, at the bottom of the fall, with salmon writhing across their mouths, and generally pay the penalty of their lives for thus intruding into the *preserve* of the lords of the creation. I have shot several.

During spring-tides, when the weather is fine, this salmon-leap attracts a great number of spectators. As the water rises the fish begin to leap—perhaps, a couple of hundred in an hour. The young ones very often miscalculate the direction they should take, leaping perpendicularly out of the water, and, of course, falling back immediately. But the older and wiser fish, many of which, no doubt, have been up before, and are better mathematicians, manage differently. These dart to the crest of the cataract, in a line with the curve of the falling mass, and there cling for some seconds, wriggling themselves into the torrent. In this very difficult position they can only work on the water with the pectoral and ventral fins; the force of their powerful tail, by which they had sprung from the bottom, being now lost in beating the air. Many, notwithstanding, succeed—dip into the water at the top and shoot up the river; but the great majority fail, and after a gallant struggle are tumbled back into the pool.

After the great leap up a fall the fish rest during several hours in the first gentle current they meet, before proceeding farther on their journey. Some Naturalists have estimated the first day's voyage of a salmon, at twenty miles; but it is plain that the distance must depend on the nature of the stream. If the river is rapid the fish's stages must be short, and *vice versa*. Very soon after salmon enter the fresh water a great change for the worse takes place in the condition of the animal—the skin, which is a correct index of the fish's condition, changes from a silvery white to a tinge of reddish brown, and then to a dirty black brown. The firmness of the muscles softens; the curd between their layers disappears and the cutaneous fat is absorbed—the appetite for food ceases, and the salmon emaciates daily. At length the flesh loses all its nutritive qualities as human food, and becomes, to a certain extent, unwholesome, or even poisonous. This deterioration is connected with the due development of the reproductive organs.

The food of salmon in the sea has been a subject of much controversy amongst Naturalists. It has been averred that they live there chiefly on the eggs of the *asterias glacialis*, or cross fish, one of the *entomostraca*, or testaceous insects. Now, from the animal's teeth, one might think he lived on more substantial food than almost microscopic ova. There is evidence that cannot be doubted, that sand-eels and smelts have been found in the stomachs of fish fresh caught, both in the Durness Frith, in Sutherlandshire, Scotland, and at Gaspé, in Lower Canada.

After entering the fresh water, it has again been a question, whether these fish eat at all, as the stomachs of many individuals have been opened at different times by various: persons, and nothing could be discovered in them.

According to my experience, the case stands thus. When they first quit the salt water they eat greedily enough—jump at flies of every description without hesitation—devour worms, grasshoppers, and even small fish. In the lakes of Killarney they are caught under these circumstances by trolling, both with natural and artificial minnows. I have found in a dozen instances the larvae of insects, remains of earthworms, grasshoppers, butterflies, and various kinds of flies, in the stomachs of salmon caught soon after quitting the sea. But, after a month or six weeks' stay in the rivers, when they begin to pair, the fish cease to eat, and then appear to be able to live for several weeks without any food whatever.

There is a ford on the Esk, about a mile to the eastward of the town of Donegal, and near the scene of my memorable rencontre with the bull, which, in my young days was a favourite resort of salmon in the breeding season. Here the bottom consists of loose gravel, the stream flows gently, and in ordinary states of the river the water is about twelve or fourteen inches deep. Concealed in a thicket at the root of some willows on the bank, I have at this place, on more than twenty occasions, watched for hours the interesting manoeuvres of the fish.

With admirable instinct these creatures never select a stream that is likely to dry up. It is essential, I believe, that the bed or nest of the ova should be at the bottom of running water of moderate depth: not in too strong a current, which, during floods, would be likely to carry off and destroy the deposit—nor in a stagnant part of the river where a mud sediment and the want of water sufficiently aerated might choke the embryo brood.

When the place is chosen both fish set to work to scoop out a proper nest for the ova, and on every occasion I noticed that the female commenced the operation, as she had in all probability acted as quarter mistress in selecting the site of the bed. She is easily distinguished from the male by her large and matronly size, as he is conspicuous by the curious hooked spur projecting upwards from the centre of the lower jaw. The female, then, in singular analogy with the hen-bird, begins to make her nest by digging into the gravel with her belly and tail, and sometimes poking a refractory pebble out of the way with her nose. The male fish all the time keeps watch in the immediate neighbourhood of his wife; and although nature has denied him the power of serenading her with a song, after the fashion of the cock-bird, our gallant *salmo* does not the less tenderly guard the privacy of his spouse, but swims round her in a protecting circle to prevent interlopers from disturbing her in her interesting employment.

When the lady-fish has worked long enough, which may be about half an hour, she rests for a little, and the attentive husband takes her place and goes on with the digging—she then circles round and watches over him in her turn. Indeed there is much moral interest excited by these proceedings; and I may add, that the reciprocal punctuality and affection with which this labour of parental providence is carried on by the silent pair, is worthy of all imitation by more exalted husbands and wives.

The bed for the ova is a trench four or five feet long and a foot and a half, or thereabouts, in breadth and depth. Soon after the roe and milt are deposited by the parent fish, they commence simultaneously covering it up with the gravel they had previously excavated with so much toil; and this appears a comparatively easy operation. I noticed that both fish remained in the vicinity of the nest all the day, but were not visible next morning, nor during the next day. The bed of the ova, when completed, looks like a child's grave before the turf is laid on.

European salmon generally spawn in October or November, and the ova remain in their bed of gravel about one hundred and forty days. The increasing heat of March and April then vivifies the brood, and the young tadpole-fish work their way by degrees out of the nest, with the filmy envelope of the egg, like an umbilical cord, still adhering to them. They grow with great rapidity, eat with voracity, and will jump at a dragon-fly as big as one of themselves. In the latter end of April and the beginning of May they gradually drop down the rivers to the sea, and are generally clear of the fresh water by the first week in June. By September they will have grown to grilses of three or four pounds weight.

The condition of the parent-fish after spawning is very deplorable, for they then become so weak and lean as scarcely to be able to resist the current of the river, and ordinarily seek the repose of some deep hole where they may remain quiet, and to a certain extent recover their strength. But they continue languid and torpid during the winter, in a condition little better than that of the hibernating animals. From the great emaciation of the body the head appears disproportionately large, and looks as if it belonged to another fish. The flesh is white, or of a dirty yellow colour; tasteless and unhealthy. When hooked by the angler, under these circumstances, they are quite passive and helpless, and suffer themselves to be dragged almost unresistingly to the shore. In early spring they fall down the rivers, and, like other valetudinarians, repair to the sea for the recovery of their health.

There is a peculiarity in the instincts of salmon worthy of notice, *viz*: their invariable habit of returning from unknown distances and depths of ocean to the streams where they were bred. They may be forced by stress of weather, or the pursuit of some of their natural enemies, into the mouth of a strange river, like a ship drives by a storm into a hostile port, but the vast majority find their way back to their native waters. Their local memory would appear to extend to food also; and, probably, the reason they take the fly so well on first leaving the sea, where they never meet with one, is a confused recollection of the habits of their youth.

Salmon, like many other animals, are subject to the attacks of parasitical enemies, which cling to their skin or infest their intestines. I have repeatedly caught fish, fresh from the sea, with the *monoculus piscinus* adhering to their skin. This insect drops off after a day or two's residence in the fresh water; but they often pick up another still more troublesome companion in the rivers,—the *lernaea salmonea*, which clings to the gill-covers, and often materially obstructs the breathing of the fish. They are freed from this annoyance as soon as they return to the sea. Tape-worms are often found in the stomach and intestines.

Trout are classed by Ichthyologists amongst the salmon-family and denominated the *salmo fario*; of which, perhaps there are a thousand varieties. The white or sea-trout, comprehending several kinds, resemble the common salmon in their form and colour, as well as their habits of migration annually, from the salt to the fresh water; but, there is reason to believe, that the great majority of the trout genera never visit the sea; as, indeed, to many of them it would be an impossibility.

CHAPTER 5

Adolescence

And now, farewell. Time unrevoked has run
His wonted course, yet what I wished is done.
By Contemplation's help, not sought in vain,
I seem t' have lived my childhood o'er again.

Cowper

I had now received a respectable country education, was decently instructed in my mother tongue, and had made a tolerable progress in the classics. I had followed the Grecian army to Troy; and after the storm tracked Ulysses and Æneas in their devious wanderings through the Mediterranean. With no little boyish vanity, I could also follow the clergyman in the lesson from the gospel and epistle in the original Greek; and I fear the feeling of self-complacency which accompanied this proceeding, was not in strict harmony with the humility usually inculcated from the pulpit. I was thus as well prepared as boys generally are, for the more severe studies of the university; and it was determined in a family conclave that I should repair to Edinburgh, study medicine at that prolific "*officina medicorum*"—graduate, and in due time establish myself as my uncle's successor.

But man can only propose—a higher power disposes. The cherished object of my own and my family's hopes and expectations was frustrated in the most cruel manner. An untimely death carried off my cousin in the bloom of her youth, and my poor heart-broken uncle soon followed her to the grave—the victim of a grief that would admit of no alleviation or comfort. As a climax, my revered mother shortly after was cut off by that relentless destroyer of all that is beautiful in form or angelic in disposition—consumption.

But why should I obtrude my early sorrows upon the public? I shall, therefore, throw a veil over them during that dismal period of twelve long and weary months, in which my young heart lay crushed, and my whole being paralysed, by the stupor and deadness of intense grief.

At length, time and the natural buoyancy of youth began to produce their usual soothing effects. A successor to my uncle established himself—the house and property were sold; and strangers soon roamed through those flowery walks, and luxuriated amidst those fragrant *parterres*, where I had enjoyed so much pure and unalloyed happiness; and which, with their departed mistress, I had hoped one day to call my own. I gave up all idea of home practice—entered Trinity College, Dublin, but with the intention of still prosecuting medical study—passed a winter in Edinburgh; and finally embarked at Newry for Liverpool, with the object of completing my surgical education in London.

The first appearance of the country in England is most attractive and fascinating to an untraveled Irish youth, in whose mind education has developed and cherished aspirations after the soft and beautiful in the moral and natural worlds, rarely realized in his own rougher and less cultivated soil. All at once, I dropped into the very bosom of Worcestershire, from the sterile mountains of Donegal; and for the first week that I spent at a friend's house, at the foot of the Malvern Hills, my sensations resembled those we may suppose to be felt on visiting a new planet, from whence all the sin, and sorrow, and disagreeable sights and sounds that infest our earth had been banished, and all was harmony, happiness, beauty and repose.

Worcestershire is a little gem amongst the English counties—none equal it, in my estimation, in its own style of quiet, but intense rural beauty. I gazed with unsated and insatiable delight, on

The rich expanse of wavy corn.

studded with luxuriant fruit trees—the magnificent and teeming orchards—the flower-embosomed cottages—emblems and abodes of cleanliness and comfort—the sleek horses in the huge wagons—the tasteful arrangement of the trees, and even the trimness of the hedges—the warm farmhouses—the stout, well clad, ingenuous and healthy peasants in their frocks—and the pretty faces that turned up from under the gipsy hats. All, together, was novel to the sight; though it appeared to me as if some such picture, now expanded before me, had, in the course of my reading, presented itself to an ardent and creative fancy.

I spent a year in London, where I was a pupil of Sir E———— H————, a great gun of his day, though by no means the best man or best surgeon in the world. I owe him little, but I owe a cleverer man, at that period young in fame, much. Even then, some thirty years ago, green and inexperienced as I was, I had a presentiment that Sir Benjamin Brodie would attain to the distinguished eminence which he has since reached.

Chapter 6

Voyage to Lisbon

The Lord hath created medicines, and he that is wise will not despise them.

    Ecclesiasticus.

Having obtained from the chirurgical wisdom of Lincoln's Inn Fields an authority to cut up all the King's liege subjects, who chose to permit me, I determined on entering the army and visiting the Peninsula; where Lord Wellington was at the time "grimly reposing" behind the lines of Torres Vedras, and waiting for a false move on the part of Massena, whom he there held in check. It is true, the Whig *quidnuncs* of the day gave me or anybody else small hope of joining the English army; except in the way of meeting it in the Bay of Biscay after being driven out of Portugal. But, notwithstanding their gloomy forebodings and craven-croaking, I resolved to try.

Accordingly, with my credentials in my hand, I went to the Horse Guards, and from thence was referred to a tribunal sitting at No. 4, Berkeley-street, Berkeley Square. The wise men on the medical bench there, having examined me, and reported that I could physic as well as bleed, I was in due course gazetted "Hospital Mate" for general service to His Majesty's Forces. The title grated on my ear at first, as cacophonous to the last degree; but one gets accustomed to disagreeable sounds. It has sunk, since, beneath the growing intelligence of the age, like any other barbarism of the middle ages.

Next day, I went to an army tailor to order my uniform. The awful black feather in my cocked-hat was calculated to raise unpleasant ideas, and I considered it scarcely fair for the Horse Guards' people to put me in mourning, prematurely, and by anticipation for any accidents amongst my patients.

I recollect that I was interrogated afterwards in Silver-Street, in Lisbon, by General P—c—ke, about this identical black feather. It was very long and pliant, and on a wet or windy day used to whisk about my eyes; so that under these circumstances, I always doubled it up into the fold of the crown of the hat to keep it out of the way. In this state the general met and accosted me—

"You are a medical officer, Sir?"

"I am, Sir."

"Then, where is your black feather, Sir?"

"There it is," I replied, flapping it across his nose. The general rode on.

About a week after my appointment, I was ordered to Portsmouth, to embark for Lisbon. I travelled in the same coach with a facetious brother *medico* bound to Cadiz, of the name of M—d—le. At the inn where we stopped to dine my companion electrified the contents of two coaches by emptying his snuff-box, more than half full, into his soup, and swallowing it with much gusto. He let me into the secret afterwards, but I could never see much to admire or imitate in burning one's mouth for the sake of exciting a little momentary wonder. It was a common trick, it seemed, to astonish strangers, and was managed by having two similar boxes, one containing snuff and the other pepper.

After waiting several days at Portsmouth for a fair wind, I sailed in the transport *Mary*, John Hogg, Master, with four officers, bound to Lisbon. I record Mr. Hogg's name for two reasons—first, he quarrelled with me one day after dinner for telling him in the course of a conversation on Heraldry, that his crest was a boar's head—and, secondly, because the said Hogg's name was the most happy example of the identity of designation and person—sound and sense—appellation and character, that I have ever had the good fortune to meet.

One clear Sunday morning in the beginning of May, 1811, we proceeded through the Needles with a fleet of three hundred sail, escorted by a frigate, the name of which I forget. The passage of such a large fleet through an intricate channel, with the beautiful Isle of Wight on one side and the richly cultivated coast on the other—the opening sea to the west, and the gradual development of canvass and increasing speed when we cleared the rocks, until at last every studding-sail was set before a fair breeze—formed a very imposing spectacle to an inexperienced eye.

All the morning and afternoon we bore down channel gallantly, and in the evening we had the pleasure of witnessing a pretty little chase. An American brig that had got permission to profit by the convoy, finding that some of the fleet were heavy sailers, and that the easterly breeze was freshening and promised to continue, took it into her head to cut our acquaintance. No doubt she thought she might leave us when she pleased, and that our frigate would hesitate at quitting the fleet to pursue her, so near night, and exposed to the chance of meeting one or two Dunkirk luggers, then supposed to be close at hand. However, for once, Jonathan reckoned without his host. As soon as the frigate saw the American making off she fired a gun, and a little after a second, without effect. Upon this the convoy which had been under single-reefed top-sails before, hoisted more sail, shook out her reefs, and dashed away in pursuit of the brig. After half an hour's trial of speed, the fugitive, finding the frigate was fast gaining on her, lay to; and, no doubt, paid dearly for the two shots—as for the scolding she got from the captain of the convoy, it was given *gratis*.

When an unfortunate landsman first goes to sea and his evil star conducts him at once, "*in medias res*" that is to say, into the Bay of Biscay, after or during a gale from the westward; sick as he may be, there is this consolation, that throughout all his after sea-life he cannot well be much worse. Our passage across this stormy bay was boisterous enough; but we were treated with several amusing scenes in the cabin, which we could enjoy after the first deadening depression of the seasickness was over.

One morning at breakfast, when I got up to manufacture some egg-cream, and had a large tea-kettle full of boiling water in one hand, and a tumbler with the egg in another, the ship gave a fearful roll, sending me and my kettle to the other side of the cabin. I then endeavoured to anchor on one of the standing berths; but, both hands being engaged, I could only use my elbow, and it would not hold, consequently, back in a second I was sent by the recoil of the vessel; and, alas! a third time launched, *nolens, volens*, on this perilous navigation. All this time my four fellow-passengers were at the table, throwing up their feet to keep out of the apprehended danger, and screaming with a sort of hysteric laughter, in which, however, fear was a principal ingredient. After two or three more turns across the cabin, I fortunately made good a landing on my chair in safety, and without spilling a drop either of the water or the cream.

Our dinners, of course, were generally enlivened by similar little interludes between the acts. Often our soup-tureen, impelled by some extraordinary ground swell, would start from its moorings, smash half a dozen decanters and tumblers in its passage, and then unrelentingly pour its scalding contents into the Vice-President's lap. Then Captain *Maunsell*, of the 39th, would exclaim—"any *more* soup Hooper?"— "Ogh, no, bad luck to you, don't you percaive I have got my *ne plus ultra*."

On the 16th May we made the Rock of Lisbon; soon after were boarded by a Portuguese pilot, and after passing the imposing array of forts at its mouth, we advanced up the Tagus with a delightful breeze and anchored off Belem Steps.

CHAPTER 7

Lisbon

Quem nao tern visto Lisbon
Nao tem visto consa boa.
Portuguese Proverb
What beauties does Lisbon first unfold.

But whoso entereth within this town
That, sheening far, eelestial seems to be,
Disconsolate will wander up and down
'Mid many things unsightly to strange ee;
For hut and palace shew like filthily:
The dingy denizens are reared in dirt;
Ne personage of high or mean degree
Doth care for cleanness of surtout or shirt,
Though shent with Egypt's plague—unkempt, unwashed, unhurt.
Childe Harold.

This scenic capital does certainly display many beauties to a stranger as his vessel drops anchor in the broad stream at its feet. There, however, he ought to stay, satisfied with distant admiration; for though all is majestic and magnificent without, all is stench and filth within.

For the first week after landing, the smell of ten thousand unsavoury odours everywhere—of every description—though many undescribable—and in various stages of concentration—by day and by night—without abatement or cessation—made me often fervently wish it had been possible to leave my nose behind me in England. For, without a doubt, a man would be happier without a nose in Lisbon.

At the period of my arrival our worthy allies, the Portuguese, had not a little cooled from the first fervour of their hospitality and civility to their English *amigos*, as was but natural; for what good nature could bear up so long with a succession of strangers, forced into their domestic privacy-draining their resources—unharmonizing with their customs and religion; and, perhaps, often requiting politeness and kindness with rudeness and disdain? My first business, naturally, was to look out for a lodging; accordingly, after reporting myself at the proper places, I repaired to the town major's office for a billet; and, having procured one, sallied forth from thence to establish myself in my quarters—a matter occasionally analogous to the dangerous invasion of an enemy's country.

Previous to leaving England, I had purchased a Portuguese grammar and dictionary, with the intention of studying hard on the voyage. But a transport in the Bay of Biscay is somewhat different from the groves of *Academus*—consequently, my progress was not great. On reaching my "*patrone's*" door—as they quaintly but kindly call one's host in Lisbon—I found on mustering my acquirements in Portuguese, that the sum total amounted to half a dozen words and one sentence—"bread," and "wine," and "water," and "fish," and "tea," and "how do you do?"

Thus accomplished, I arrived in front of a good-looking house in the Rua dos Plaçeres, in Buenos Ayres—the best part of Lisbon. I was admitted with politeness by a well-dressed servant, and shewn into an anti-chamber, where sat a gentlemanly-looking *fidalgo*, with the Maltese cross on his breast. These were favourable circumstances, and those first appearances of respectability and courtesy were not belied by the subsequent deportment of my worthy host. After the introductory bow to each other, we were both not a little puzzled to find that our literary acquirements had not furnished a mutual channel of communication. He knew about as much English as I did Portuguese, and was unacquainted with French. 'Twas true, the excellent *fidalgo* had picked up a few oaths, which he had heard amongst the English soldiers; but these expletives were not much calculated to make our ideas intelligible to each other, or to keep up a good understanding between us. In this dilemma we had recourse again to the eloquence of courtesy and the countenance—bows,

——and smiles, and sparkles of the speaking eye—

till, his knight's cross having haply suggested to me that he might understand Latin, I accosted him as well as I could in that language. Fortunately, I had been taught to pronounce it in the broad, Continental, and not the English manner—so, he understood me at once,

45

and a *medius terminus* being thus established between us, we chatted away as classically as we might on the events of the day—the "*bellum internecinum adversus Gallos*"—the great "*Dux* Wellington"—the "*exercitus Britannicus*"—the "*Rex Georgius*"—the "*spes Lusitaniae*"—and so forth, for half an hour, until we became cordial cronies, and the good old gentleman finished by inviting me to dinner.

We dined *tête à tête*, and I enjoyed my kind "*patrone's*" multiform and manifold dishes with considerable gusto, notwithstanding rather too strong a savour of the *alho*; but the calm that followed the perturbations in the Bay of Biscay was accompanied with an accommodating appetite. Although we spoke in the Roman language we did not carry our imitation of the ancients to the extent of reclining like them—

ab ovo usque ad mala,

but sat very comfortably in the *fidalgo's* well cushioned armchairs. A duck happened to be one of the dishes—the *ala* and the *crus* were easily recollected; but it puzzled us both to call to mind the exact Ciceronian for the stuffing.

By the assistance of my good host, I acquired in the course of a week as much Portuguese as relieved the Latin occasionally, or sometimes superseded it altogether. He was besides very useful to me in many other respects; acting as my guide in pointing out the lions of the Lusitanian metropolis, and introducing me to several of his friends, after our acquaintance had ripened into intimacy. He was, I believe, a true patriot—loved his country, was cordial to the English—deprecated the Convention of Cintra, of which he could not speak with patience, and abominated Junôt and the French; who had insulted him and stolen his plate and pictures. In fact, I felt then and afterwards—and still feel under the greatest obligations to this warm-hearted gentleman; and as I never could repay him in his own country, nor any other, I shall now do all in my power in the way of gratitude, by consigning the name of Don Manoel Joze Mascarenhas to the limited immortality of my book.

When I first landed I had called on Dr. B——, the principal medical officer, but he was not at home; next morning I was more fortunate, and found this gentleman—an old schoolfellow of my father—who received me as graciously as his nature permitted. After a short conversation, in the course of which he directed me to call the next morning for farther instructions; and when I had risen from the chair, preparatory to taking my leave, we were both startled by a shrill, violent, and prolonged female shriek from the upper part of the house. The principal medical officer suddenly turned as pale as a sheet; and, exclaiming, "By G—— she has killed herself!" rushed out of his office and ran upstairs. Another loud scream met his ear almost immediately, and perceptibly accelerated his steps; whilst I was left, hat in hand, deliberating whether it behoved me to disappear, or to wait for the denouement of what promised to turn out something sufficiently tragic.

I was not left long in suspense, for in two minutes a frightened female servant came running down stairs, half a dozen steps in one, and requesting me to hurry up without delay. On entering a bedchamber, I found the doctor and another servant supporting and soothing a very handsome young lady, who was pale and faint, and bleeding profusely from a wound in the left breast. As the chief *medico* was so dreadfully agitated that he could be of no use, he requested me to examine the wound and take the proper measures for dressing it and staunching the bleeding. I found that the patient had stabbed herself with a stiletto; fortunately, the point had struck against a rib and glanced off, producing a deep flesh-wound, but not penetrating the chest. She had, moreover, and it was a pity, pierced a very white and well formed bosom, and the blood was running down her side on the bed in a considerable stream. I soon succeeded in stopping the bleeding; the fair suicide was then undressed, after the usual restoratives, and put to bed. She was obstinately silent in answer to the reiterated questions of the doctor; but it appeared to me she did not receive my announcement that the wound was not fatal, in the mood to be expected from a person still determined on self-destruction, but quite the contrary.

The history of the case was this. Dr. B—— had had this lady, an extremely pretty Portuguese, living under his protection for a considerable period; but, on making preparations to embark for England, he wished to cut the connection. The overture he made to this effect was very unpalatable to his mistress, who desired to accompany him, and even hoped to be made his wife in process of time. It appeared that on the morning of my second call, there had been a recent and violent altercation between the parties. He swore she should not go with him, and she said and swore she would. The ungallant *medico* then flew into a passion, called her a fury, and a fiend, and abused her as far as his limited Portuguese would permit. In reply, she vowed she would destroy herself, and that he should have her life to answer for, and then asked pardon of the "*Virgem purissima*"—the above catastrophe was the result.

I attended the fair lady for a week. She soon recovered, and I have my own suspicions that previous to stabbing herself she had carefully studied the anatomy of the rib which her *poniard* encountered, and which saved her life. At any rate she failed in her great object—the doctor pensioned and discarded her—and she returned to the opera.

About this period there was great lack of medical assistance, both with the main allied army in the north of Portugal, and in Beresford's corps, quartered in Spanish Estramadura. The battles of Fuentes d'Onore and Albuera had filled the hospitals with wounded, and there were many sick. There chanced at the time to be a large detachment of the 11th regiment at Lisbon, preparing to join their headquarters in the north of Portugal, without a regimental medical officer. It was therefore arranged that I should embark with them for Figueras, a town at the mouth of the Mondego, and accompany them up the river to Coimbra, where I was directed to report myself and await farther orders.

CHAPTER 8

Coimbra

Doces e claras aguas do Mondego.
Camoens

The weather was fine when we embarked at Belem in the beginning of June, 1811; and we had a pleasant voyage of two days to Figueras. There, the detachment was put in flat bottomed boats, and we proceeded up the vine-banked and beautiful Mondego to Coimbra.

Coimbra, the most classical city—and seat of the only university in the kingdom; with a name unpronounceable by nine strangers out of ten—is built on a fine hill rising boldly from the broad and clear river. There is a long bridge; and on the opposite rich height are romantically pitched the Convent of St. Francisco, half-way up—and Santa Clara at the top. In fact, every hill in the beautiful environs of this ancient and celebrated city has its convent, picturesquely crowning the summit, and embosomed in groves of pine, oak, chesnut, cypress, myrtle, olive and orange trees; for the friars of the olden time had excellent judgement in the selection of good sites for their domiciles. Although they affected such utter seclusion from the world, they generally managed to perch themselves in a position that afforded a bird's-eye view of everything going on in it. I counted sixteen convents in and around Coimbra.

Having reported my arrival to Dr.T——t, then at the head of the medical staff at Coimbra, I was directed to cross to the other side of the Mondego and take charge of a ward of about a hundred poor wounded fellows, lately brought in from the front, and now quartered in the Francisco Convent. I was also ordered to get a billet in a hamlet near the convent.

The second morning after I had established myself, in passing under some fine chestnut trees near the convent gate, I saw a good-looking Portuguese lad lying on his back in the shade, taking a comfortable *siesta*. It immediately occurred to me that I wanted a servant, and that here was the very *"criado"* I required, dosing away his time for want of a master; accordingly, by way of introduction, I touched him gently in the side with the toe of my boot. Antonio started up—collected a frown on his handsome brow at the freedom I had taken; but strangled it instantly and put a smile in its place, when he saw my red coat and cocked-hat. We then entered into amicable conversation, and I asked after his acquirements. Although he could neither make spatter-dashes nor play on the fiddle, like Sterne's La Fleur—he said he could cook, and brush my clothes, and polish my boots, and groom a horse. He had no certificates, for he had never been in service—but he had an honest as well as comely face; and trusting to an ingenuous manner and this natural recommendation, I hired him at once—appointed him my *Major Domo* and *factotum*, and directed him to look after my rations.

When my morning hospital duties were over, I strolled up the river side to the *"Quinta das Lagrimas,"* and thence to the *"Fonte dos Armores"*—the former the traditionary abode, and the latter the scene of the murder, of the celebrated Ignes de Castro. The Fountain, running over marble full of red spots, still believed to be the marks left by her blood, is surrounded by some magnificent cypresses—a tree that is peculiarly umbrageous and beautiful in Portugal.

The story of Ignes de Castro is one of those historical facts that are stranger, more affecting and more appalling than fiction. The disinterment of the murdered lady—the attiring of the corpse in royal robes—the coronation—the homage of the nobility—the pomp of the final sepulture of Alcobaca—are incidents strangely sublime—the triumph of love over death!

> *De noite em doces sonhos que mentiam—*
> *Do die em pensainentos que vouvam;*
> *E quanto em fim cuidava, e quanto via*
> *Eram tudo memorias de alegria.*
>
> Camoens.

It is not very usual to jump the one step *from the sublime to the ridiculous*, but it is common enough to descend from this elevation to the occupations and amusements of ordinary life. Thus, after the contemplation of the sad story of Ignes, in returning along the river my eye was attracted by some lively fish playing about and glancing in the water. Instantly my sentimentalities took wing—the old angling predilections resumed their ascendency—I hastened home—put in order the cane-rod that I always carried with me—repaired to the river-side—began to fish—and in an hour succeeded in persuading a dozen good sized dace to accompany me home to dinner.

I found that my valet had not overrated his culinary qualifications. He made some tolerable soup out of the tough ration beef, and fried the fish nicely with the *azeite*, fresh drawn from the olive trees on the neighbouring hill. A bullock's heart roasted, was also very properly cooked; and when the cloth was removed I sipped my ration wine philosophically over a dessert of delicious grapes and oranges, with a full view of the city—the college, the numerous convents—the gushing river, and the Sierra de Busaco from my window. Thinks I to myself this is mighty pleasant campaigning.

Next day I visited the university, where I was much disappointed; as from the dispersion of the professors and students by the recent French invasion, everything appeared to be going to decay. The library—chemical apparatus, and those of natural philosophy, seemed in a deplorable condition—many of the public lectures had ceased, and there were said not to be more than a hundred students. The few present supported themselves by manufacturing tooth-picks, and hence were nick-named "*Politos.*"

The observatory appeared to be in better order than any other part—there were several good French instruments. The view from the western side, embracing a long reach of the Mondego, backed by lofty *Sierras*, with the Quinta das Lagrimas, the Fonte dos Amores, the Santa Clara and Francesco on the glorious hill opposite—the convent-crowned hills, the river, bridge, aqueduct, and city, in the foreground—is very magnificent.

Part of the Santa Clara Convent had been given up for the use of the sick and wounded, but the remainder was occupied by the nuns. I frequently attended the chapel to hear these sisters' singing, which certainly was admirable; but, so many heretics being in their immediate neighbourhood, they appeared to be preserved with more than ordinary care from all possibility of the most harmless intercourse. Even the usual *grille* and turning box were blocked up. However, to console us for this privation, report said they were mostly old ladies, with one young beauty, one acknowledged beauty amongst them, who, crossed in love, had thrown herself into the convent. Such is the witchery of a fair face, even an ideal one, over all the senses, that in listening to the choir in the chapel, I always associated Donna Theodora's idea with one voice pre-eminently sweet; although, for aught I know to the contrary, the said beautiful lady might have a note like a peahen.

When I was in Coimbra there was a fountain in the garden of the Santa Cruz Convent of Augustine Friars, within the city, which all the English officers greatly admired; for it was a pleasing and cool retreat to the convalescents from the great heat of the town. The fountain was a circular sheet of water, some thirty yards in diameter, surrounded by a verdant wall of clipped cypress, forty or fifty feet high; and having a little circular island in the middle, on which grew one orange tree, worthy of the garden of the Hesperides. There was a comfortable seat at the bottom of the verdant enclosure for the refreshment of the *Padres*; and, to do the whole Santa Cruz establishment but justice, they threw their gates open in a very handsome manner to the English. They permitted us to bathe in the fountain; and our common habit was to swim round the tiny island until we were tired, then land and return loaded with as many oranges as we could manage to carry in our teeth.

The country around Coimbra, on both sides of the Mondego, is rich and beautiful; probably, unsurpassed by any district in the Peninsula; certainly by none which I have seen. The slopes rise into hills softly and gracefully; the acclivities richly covered with Indian corn, vineyards and olive grounds, mingled with groves and clumps of tall forest trees; and the crowning *quinta*, or convent, embowered in its deep mass of foliage, at the top. Next to the view from the College observatory, that from the Santa Clara Convent is the most extensive, and I have stood for hours feasting my eyes with the splendid prospect, containing all the elements of the finest landscape-picture, that lay before me; and bounded in the distance by ranges of mountains, pre-eminent amongst which, though at the greatest distance, was the Sierra de Estralla; the "*Mons Herminius*" of antiquity.

But the valley of the Mondego, so lovely to the eye and so rich in soil and in natural products, has yet its drawbacks; and they are neither few nor unimportant. During the winter the most frightful floods, bearing with them stones and rocks from the mountains, ravage the banks and lay all the low country under water. In fact, there is an inundation for three or four months, followed by extensive malaria, when the sun gains power and the wet surface begins to dry in the spring.

Coimbra, like all Portuguese towns, except Portalegre, is dirty, even to the taste of the most fastidious of the race of swine. These uninteresting animals had been much thinned by the French invasion; but in the choice pasture the city afforded at this time, they bade fair to be soon as flourishing as ever. Portuguese pigs, universally, are the ugliest quadrupeds imaginable—tall, and gaunt, and melancholy; and looking like what we might fancy Don Quixotte would be, touched by the wand of Circe.

Few rivers can produce frogs in greater abundance than the Mondego; the winter inundation affording this noisy fraternity great facilities in the breeding season. In the quiet hamlet where I resided, I was screened by its situation and the shade of the fine trees from the great heat of the town; but I was in the very focus of the frogs. When I awoke, stunned by the terrific croak, croak, croak, of some billions of these reptiles, it seemed to me that all this tremendous uproar could not be an occurrence of ordinary seasons; and as I could not sleep, I thought I might as well form some theory to account for it. After two or three hours puzzling my brain, I found out what satisfied me then, as the veritable cause of all the uproar. In the year 1811, the whole nation of frogs wore keeping an universal jubilee, in consequence of the recent expulsion from the kingdom of their cannibal enemies, the French.

Coimbra at this time contained nearly a thousand British sick and wounded, so that there was a fine field for practice. We had many bad surgical cases, and not a few extraordinary recoveries after terrible round-shot wounds. Amongst these there was a patient of mine, a grenadier of the 77th regiment, who had been wounded at the affair of El Bordon, when this regiment and the 5th Foot behaved so beautifully, retreating in square before overwhelming numbers of French cavalry, never losing their formation, and carrying off their wounded over three or four leagues of open country. A cannon-ball had struck him on the back, but, as it was nearly spent, his knapsack and the tin vessel over it had turned the shot out of its direct course; but it had ploughed its way downwards, carrying the tin with it, and cutting everything soft of the poor fellow's hinder parts sheer off as clean as with a carving knife. There was great bleeding at the time, but he fainted, was carried off by his comrades, and the nearest surgeon tied up the large arteries, when he recovered. He was soon after sent down to Coimbra.

The cure was necessarily tedious, but it was at length happily completed; and nature had furnished him with new skin over the enormous wound about as extensive as the hide of a calf. When I left Coimbra he was beginning to move about slowly on crutches; still very lame from the great loss of muscle. At parting he expressed much gratitude for my attentions, and in return I wished he might get a good pension and a soft-bottomed chair for the remainder of his life.

In the month of July, apprehensions being entertained at head quarters that another retreat on the lines might be necessary, from the junction of the French army of the south and that of Portugal, orders arrived to clear the hospitals and send the sick to Lisbon. Accordingly they were broke up, and a large detachment of two hundred was placed under my charge. We embarked on the river, were put on board a transport at Figueras, and arrived without accident at Lisbon.

CHAPTER 9

Cintra

The horrid crags, by toppling convent crown'd;
The cork trees hoar that clothe the snaggy steep—
The mountain moss by scorching skies embrown'd,
The sunken glen whose sunless shrubs must weep;
The tender azure of the unruffled deep—
The orange tints that gild the greenest bough;
The torrents that from hill to valley leap—
The vine on high, the willow branch below—
Mix'd in one mighty scene with varied beauty glow.

                                                   Byron.

One thinks one's self at Cintra transported to a planet very different from this homely earth. It is assuredly, at the least, one of the most extraordinary spots upon its surface; and though it offers to the eye the most singular scenic paradoxes, yet, after a little observation, everything appears in fine keeping.

I sailed three times close under the mountain, and spent two long summer days luxuriating amongst the gelid retreats of Cintra. Nothing can be more striking than the abrupt transitions of scenery; the alternations of rich landscapes with overwhelming desolation; the darkness of the profound ravines and the lovely sunny slopes at the top; the vast rocks; the cascades; the gardens teeming with golden fruit; the oak and cork forests; the palaces and convents; the vast conical mountains; the immeasurable view of the Atlantic from their peaked summits; all is majestic and glorious. Alas! why should human crime mar the magnificence of nature; that rude cross surrounded by its cairn of rough stones tells but too plainly of a recent murder!

My first care after returning to Lisbon, was to visit my fine old "*patrone*" the Knight of Malta. There was an officer of the German Legion quartered in the house, but he was under orders to set out for the army the next day. In the meantime the excellent Don Manoel directed Antonio to go for my baggage forthwith, and I soon found myself comfortably re-established in my former habitation.

In the course of a couple of days I was directed to do duty at an hospital, under the charge of a German staff surgeon, whose name it is not necessary to mention. I soon found that my worthy Teutonic chief was much fonder of *schnapps* than of surgery; and from keeping late hours, not particularly punctual in his morning visits at the hospital; in fact, sometimes staying away altogether three or four days. This was exactly what I wished, for it gave me the real management and most of the practice of the establishment. I recollect that on one of the few occasions when we met in the morning, I pointed out to him a man with a bad wound in the leg, which would not heal, and required amputation to save his life. The vinous staff surgeon, unfortunately, was not in the best operating condition, for his hand shook sadly; so he deferred the matter till the next day.

At the appointed time the jovial German was again absent: after waiting for some time in vain, I took off the limb myself, with the assistance of a smart orderly. The day after, the staff surgeon and myself went round the wards together, and when we came to the patient, who had worn for some time, what is technically called a cradle, to protect his leg from the weight of the bedclothes, and which now concealed the stump; he accosted him—"Well, my goot frind, how duz your leck?"

"Faith, your honour, I was aised of it yesthurday, and I now only feels a thrifle of a pain in aich of my toes."

The doctor stared a little, but was satisfied with my explanation, and we then went to his quarters to lunch. Afterwards he amused me with his violoncello on which he played skilfully; we dined together and went to Salitre's theatre in the evening.

Notwithstanding their "nasal twang" the Portuguese are a musical people, and had the merit of first appreciating and fostering Catalani. At this time, however, there was a great dearth of musical talent in Lisbon, and the performances at the Opera were below mediocrity. The smaller theatres were wretched affairs, which no modest woman could visit on account of the constant and disgusting indecency of the performances.

I presume that everybody conversant with the local peculiarities of

Lisbon, is aware of the occurrence of periodical nocturnal rains there regularly throughout the year, beginning between ten and eleven o'clock, p. m., and lasting, generally, about two hours. One remarkable peculiarity is, that the fall of rain is limited to the city and its suburbs; though showers of the same description, occurring at the same period, are common in other large cities throughout the kingdom. The confinement of the rains to the towns is a beneficent arrangement of nature, for they are believed to be very prejudicial to vegetation.

Another singularity connected with them—a phenomenon not easily explained by any atmospheric laws with which we are acquainted—is a kind of warning or premonition before they take place; in fact, a rumbling in the clouds, somewhat resembling the human voice, and most probably of electric origin. As the inhabitants of Lisbon much dislike to be caught in this rain, and have been, indeed, morbidly sensitive of strange sounds in the air ever since the great earthquake of 1755, which was preceded by noises of this kind, they are always on the alert about the time of the expected setting in of the nightly shower; and as soon as the thunder mutters some such cabalistic sound as "*agua vem!*" a great sensation is felt in the streets, and everybody houses himself with great despatch. Immediately the rains descend in torrents, particularly in the narrow and lofty streets.

About ten days after my arrival in Lisbon, a brother *medico* and myself were returning from the Opera about twelve o'clock, dressed in our best coats. Not being fully aware of the meteorological laws of this country, nor apprised of the premonitory serial countersign, we had the misfortune to be caught suddenly in a very heavy shower—in fact, a water-spout, that sadly spoiled our scarlet.

Few mortals approach half a century without having to lament numerous youthful indiscretions. One of my early follies I may be permitted to narrate.

About the month of August, 1811, some general order of Lord Wellington respecting a certificate from the principal medical officer, before the monthly allowance for a servant could be drawn from the Commissariat by the junior medical officers, excited great wrath among the young doctors. The obnoxious order directed that this allowance should only be issued if the P. M. O. considered that a servant was absolutely necessary—an awkwardness of expressing the order, probably attributable to the bungling of some clerk at headquarters. However, the *medicos* took fire at what they considered an insult, and a meeting of "Hospital Mates" took place at Lecor's Hotel, to deliberate upon the subject. The medical staff at Lisbon was strong at this time—the meeting was attended by sixty or seventy persons, and I happened to be placed in the Chair.

After a prolonged discussion and much impassioned dilating on our grievances, branching out into very miscellaneous oratory, a committee was appointed by ballot to draw up a petition and remonstrance, to the Commander of the Forces against the recent order. The committee, of which I was a member, *ex officio*, carried into effect the directions of the meeting, and submitted the result of their labours to their constituents at another general meeting held at the same place a week after. The petition was there approved, and it was unanimously resolved that it should be presented by the committee to Dr. B——, the P. M. Officer in Lisbon, with a request to forward it to Lord Wellington's Military Secretary. After the business was thus despatched to our entire satisfaction, we had a hot supper, and finished the evening with singing and jollification.

At the appointed hour the committee waited on Dr. B—— with the petition and remonstrance, which we considered quite a *chef d'oeuvre* of composition. The doctor was the gentleman whose mistress had stabbed herself, and who was now waiting the arrival of his successor to embark for England. He received us civilly, put on his spectacles and proceeded to read our laboured document, which we were nearly certain he would approve, and even admire. When he had done he coolly replaced his glasses in their case, and then accosted us—"Why, d—— your young bloods, you fools—what have we here—a petition and remonstrance to the Commander of the Forces from a parcel of d—— 'Hospital Mates'—be off, and be d—— to you—you may think yourselves lucky that I do no more than quash your folly—thus!" And with that he tore our eloquent appeal into a thousand pieces and flung them in our faces.

When we had left the house and proceeded a few yards down the street, a messenger called me back. The doctor then addressed me—"and *you*, Sir, have been such a d—— ignoramus and blockhead as to become president of this wise deliberative meeting, and to sign your name first to your remonstrance—why. Sir, if I forwarded the petition *your* commission would not be worth that snap—the others might be overlooked, but you would be made an example of, by G—!" He then, in a more friendly tone, pointed out to me the impropriety and danger of bodies of officers meeting to deliberate without lawful authority. The doctor soon changed the subject—asked about my hospital—laughed a little concerning the convivial propensities of my immediate superior, the German—told me my patient, the fair suicide, had been dismissed—asked me to dinner the next day, and we parted very good friends.

That evening a meeting was summoned at the hotel to report proceedings respecting the petition, and we had a very full attendance. I took the Chair, and began with as much power of face as I could muster, to relate the transactions at the P. M. O's. office—repeating his precise words and mimicking his manner as well as I could. When I finished, there was, first, a murmur of disapprobation, which, however, did not last long, but was soon drowned in a loud and general laugh. It was then proposed and carried;

1st. That the consideration of our grievances should be postponed *sine die*;

2nd. That an inquisition should be forthwith made into the quantity of *collares* in the cellar; and;

3rd. That a large instalment should be mulled and produced immediately. The weather abounded in radical heat calling for corresponding moisture—the wine was delicious and not strong—temperance societies had not yet been born—the night was short and the morning sun lighted us to our homes.

CHAPTER 10

Quarrel with an Alkaldi

————*animam ne crede puellis*
Namque est faeminea tutior unda fide.
Petronius.

Exactly opposite to Don Manoel's house there resided two good-looking Portuguese girls, who passed the greater part of their time, when the shade of the house or the cool of the evening permitted, in their handsome gilded balcony. I watched their manoeuvres with a good deal of attention, and found that their principal amusement consisted in playing tricks on the Gallegos, or Gallician water-carriers, passing beneath, with their little painted barrels on their shoulders. No sooner did a Gallego approach than these damsels would accost him—"*tio! tio!*" Uncle—uncle—the familiar term used to the lower classes. The man would stop and look up; then—I shudder whilst I relate a deed so unladylike and atrocious—the playful girls would giggle and spit in his eye. The water-carrier would retort by a squirt from the pipe of his barrel about the ladies' ankles, and this was considered great fun on both sides. Yet, my "*patrone*" told me these ladies were of respectable family and irreproachable character.

As our respective balconies were only separated by a narrow street, I soon introduced myself, and we generally had a little conversation every fine evening, which was wont to become more animated as the increasing darkness screened us from observation. Mutual compliments were then interchanged; I praised the brilliancy of the ladies' eyes, and their fine persons; unusual in Lisbon, where dumpiness is a common characteristic of the women. I perceived that my lively neighbours were much at a loss to discover a laudable quality about me, and were obliged to content themselves by saying, "*vos merced tem minto bonitas dentes*"—you have good teeth.

Except occasionally playing a *modinha* set to music, on the guitar, I firmly believe these girls never read, nor worked, nor drew, nor visited, nor went out, except to church; nor did anything but lounge through the house, look out of the windows, loll on the couches—make love when they could, and amuse themselves with the Gallegos. And such I found out was the general routine of unmarried female life amongst the higher classes in Lisbon.

Don Manoel, unlike the Portuguese, generally, was fond of boating, and we often made little excursions on the river in the delightful Lisbon evenings. Nothing can be finer than the views from the river for an extent of nine or ten miles—the city rising grandly and amphitheatrically from the water on one side, and the bold and beautiful banks on the other. One evening we stopped suddenly when approaching the quay, and my "*patrone*" exclaimed—"On this spot where the water is now deep, my grandfather and grandmother, with a family of four children, stood during the earthquake on dry ground, and in fancied security, with a crowd of other fugitives from the ruins—when the water suddenly rose and engulfed them all;—my father was the only individual saved out of the family, by clinging to a boat—all the rest, with two hundred people, perished."

Few earthquakes on record were so awfully destructive as that of 1755. It happened about nine o'clock in the morning of All Saints' day, the 1st of November, when a large proportion of the population were assembled in the churches. In five minutes sixty thousand people perished. Even in those churches that partially escaped, fire destroyed what the earthquake had spared—the numerous lights employed in the gorgeous Roman Catholic ritual were thrown down, and set fire to everything inflammable around; and in the frightful confusion of the moment, the only thought was personal safety.

The Spanish court and nation behaved well on this sad occasion, and succours for the distressed city flowed in with liberality. It is pleasing to find that our Country—always in the first rank of beneficence when misfortune calls for aid—was conspicuous amongst the European nations for the large sums voted by the legislature and raised by private subscription to relieve the misery of the wretched inhabitants. We can scarcely conceive anything more intensely distressing than the state of the city for a year after the earthquake. So utterly prostrated were the people, that but for the exertions of a great man and a great minister, Pombal, they would have left the ruins of their doomed city for ever and emigrated in a body to Brazil.

Lisbon and the whole of Portugal are, and have been from time immemorial, subject to earthquakes—most of these have been harmless, and only three or four have done mischief. The country is pierced by numerous hot-springs, shewing that a magazine of fire exists at no great distance from the surface. One evening, as Don Manoel and myself were taking our coffee, a shock occurred which was only of short duration, but sufficiently lively to jingle the cups on the table where they stood, and set a Mandarin figure shaking his head very gravely at the phenomenon.

According to my *"patrone's"* statement, the French, when in occupation of Lisbon, must have behaved infamously ill, and pillaged openly and universally. They seized all the church plate they could find, and were not particular in respecting what belonged to private individuals. The forced contributions exacted by Junôt were enormous—Don Manoel had paid at one time four thousand *crusadoes*, and smaller sums on two or three occasions—he had also lost part of his plate; but when he discovered the rapacity of the new masters of the kingdom, he secreted and saved the remainder. His pictures suffered—but he cared nothing for any that had been taken away, except one *Murillo*—a scripture-piece which he prized highly.

Butchers' meat at this time was of very indifferent quality in Lisbon, but there was an excellent fish-market; and Antonio, who had conducted himself remarkably well hitherto, was a good fish-cook, so that ichthyophagism was the order of the day. As to wine, we had the strong white wine from the south shore of the Tagus—the *Portofeitoria* red wine—*Calcavellos*, and the delicious Portuguese Claret—*Collares*—all very reasonable—*Champaigne*, Claret, Port, Madeira and Sherry, were to be had, but at such prices as did not suit my finances—nor did the hot and heady nature of most of them harmonize any better with my humble and undisciplined taste. I luxuriated amongst the grapes and oranges, as most strangers do on a first visit to Lisbon.

After a residence of four months, spent most agreeably in the Portuguese capital, I was ordered to Aldea Galega, a village on the other side of the Tagus at the commencement of the high-road to Elvas. There was a strong detachment of Royal Marines quartered there, of which I got medical charge. In the course of a few weeks the three officers and the greater part of the detachment were withdrawn and only a sergeant's guard remained. By some *mal-arrangement* in the Inspector of Hospitals' department, I was not relieved, although I represented that there was nothing to do. Here then I continued in the double capacity of principal medical officer and commandant, having under my authority a commissariat clerk, a sergeant, twelve marines and Antonio.

Gentlemen who have had the honour of being born in my country are, generally, represented as great adorers of the softer sex. There may be some truth in the "impeachment," although much exaggeration; at any rate, if Irishmen are a little *ultra* in this matter, they know that it is expected of them, and that they must keep up the national character. It is not their fault so much as that of the dear ladies, who would be, no doubt, offended by any other line of conduct, and who look on innocent gallantry in an Irishman, as natural and decorous as gravity in a Quaker.

I happened to occupy a very good quarter in Aldea Galega, in fact, the best house in the town; and what was better, there was an extremely pretty young girl in it, named Theodora, the daughter of my host, with whom I could not well help falling in love, being the only British officer in the town. Accordingly, we commenced a vigorous flirtation, though under the disadvantage of an inmate in the house, a maiden aunt of the fair Theodora; who, as nearly the last of the almost extinct tribe of *Duennas*, concentrated in her breast and deportment all their watchfulness and malignity.

But love laughs at *Duennas*. My trusty Antonio conveyed one day a note to my mistress, written in choice Portuguese, filled with the usual amatory hyperboles and soft fibs at which Jove is said to laugh; and concluding by soliciting a short meeting on the stairs, that I might, if only for a moment, hear the dulcet sounds of her voice—(our amour hitherto having been confined to the eyes)—and assure her how much I was devoted to her charms, &c. &c. &c. I took the liberty of enclosing her a fishing-hook, fastened to a long thread, which I implored her to employ in dropping me an answer at night from her bedchamber window, immediately above mine, and to preserve it carefully, as affording us a medium of future correspondence. The old song says—

> *I took it in my head*
> *To write my Love a letter,*
> *But, alas! she cannot read,*
> *And I like her all the better.*

So my poor Theodora could not read; but she either found some female confidant to read my *billet* for her, or with her sex's sagacity conjectured the mystic meaning of the hook; for, as soon as it became dark, down came the line with a beautiful red rose fastened by the stem, which the most obtuse understanding could not avoid considering—"*le premier gage d'amour*"

We met on the stairs. I exhausted my stock of Portuguese in whispers of love and devotion; and the amiable Theodora had just acknowledged in return that she esteemed and loved the "*valorosos Inglezez;*" and had blushed no insuperable objection to myself in particular; when the old Hecate, her aunt, suddenly made her appearance. Poor Theodora was thunderstruck—she wept, and embraced her aunt's knees, and kissed her shrivelled hand, and begged hard for concealment of the matter from papa. I implored the old lady by the most moving considerations I could shape into decent Portuguese, to be good-natured and propitious to our mutual flame, assuring her that my intentions were honourable, and even daring to compliment her on the kindness of her heart and benevolence of her countenance, although, in truth, she had the visage of a Gorgon. But flattery and entreaty were equally lost labour. With what was intended for a withering scowl, she called me a "*maldito eretico*" and seizing the trembling girl by the arm, she hurried her to her apartment by the application of five or six terrific slaps on the back. Notwithstanding this cruel treatment, the hook and line brought me that night another rose, and I returned a note as affectionate as possible.

But treachery was at work. Next day the *Juiz de Fora*, or chief magistrate of the town, sent for me, and after embracing me much more cordially than I wished—for he was redolent of tobacco and garlic—he made a thousand apologies for the painful necessity he was under of changing my quarter; but, as a compensation, he would give me a billet on the next best house in the town. The fact was, he assured me, a Portuguese general officer was every hour expected at Aldea Galega, and the best quarter in the place, which I occupied, was for him. Hereupon I remonstrated, and argued that it was not a little hard to turn out the chief doctor and commandant, permanently quartered in the town, for the accommodation of any brigadier for only one night. The *Juiz* was superfluously polite—he bowed and smirked, and used the blandest language, but concluded by saying how much-soever he regretted the necessity—I *must* turn out.

After half an hour's debate he continued inexorable. I then waxed wrath, and I fear, swore lustily, that I defied him and his friend the general, *à l'outrance*, and would not budge an inch. The fat little magistrate then flushed up into a towering passion—looked very livid and apoplectic, and swore by one-and-twenty thousand *Diabos* he would oust me, *vi et armis*, and so we parted.

But the commandant of Aldea Galega, who suspected trickery, was not to be bullied out of his good lodging and the vicinity of his *carissima*. I immediately posted a marine sentry on the door of the house, with specific directions to defend the garrison and repel any attack from the enemy. For two days the post was thus held by regular reliefs—but no general made his appearance—in fact, no general came at all; for it was all a plot to turn me out of the house, probably to break off the little *liason* with Theodora. So I triumphed over the conspirators and dismissed my sentry; but my poor mistress was sent out of the way and I saw her no more.

By this time I had purchased a good-looking Portuguese horse, and found, to my great satisfaction, that my trusty Antonio groomed him well and turned him out very smartly. The rides around the town were pleasant and the road dry, but rather sandy. The umbrageousness of the fine cork tree forests on the road to Elvas afforded thick shade and cool rides, even in the hottest part of the day. There is a high hill commanding an extensive view of Lisbon and the Tagus on this road, which used generally to be the boundary of my excursions. On the top was a marble pillar, with a coarsely sculptured image of the Virgin and an infant Jesus in her arms, apparently the objects of long and fervent devotion, and now toppling to their fall from the effects of it. For, at the part of the shaft which the lips of kneeling devotees could reach, the marble was deeply eroded, by more than two-thirds of its substance, from the ardent salutations of the travellers. To preserve the sacred effigies at the top, a kissing circle of brass round the worn part of the shaft was become indispensably necessary.

In the beginning of December, 1811, I was once more ordered to Lisbon, where I found my old apartments, at Don Manoel's, occupied by a brother *medico*—consequently looked out for lodgings elsewhere; and as I had been lately tired of idleness at Aldea, I volunteered to be resident attendant in a convent full of sick near the Campo d'Ourike. 'Tis true, when on the other side of the Tagus I had been studying Portuguese hard, and had ridden all over the country, and sauntered amongst the vineyards, and assisted the civil peasants in pruning their vines, as far as a penknife would go, and kept a journal and made love besides—still, isolated as I was there, time had moved with leaden sandals, and as if he used the handle of his scythe for a staff, with a spike in the end, which stuck in the ground at each step he took. The experience of my life, as of all rational people, proves that the lazy Sybarite, who first exclaimed "*dolec cosa far niente*," told a gigantic fib.

The Christmas day of 1811, at Lisbon, was one of the most brilliant and beautiful days that the sun ever saw, and he has seen not a few in his time. The geraniums, and roses, and *balsams*, and *passifloras*, were blooming in the open air: and the temperature was as warm as May in England, though the sky was much clearer, and there was no comparison between its delicate and rich azure and our muddy blue. I enjoyed the delicious time the more for having sat up half the preceding night, witnessing the gorgeous ceremonies of Christmas Eve in the "*Igreja da Renya.*" The church had been then crowded almost to suffocation; and the heat and confinement—the fumes of incense and the innumerable lights, mixing with the un-aromatic exhalations from four or five thousand garlic-eating people—were good preparations for enjoying the pure Atlantic breeze, the magnificent prospects and rich sunshine of Cintra.

On my return I dined with a medical friend residing in the San Jeronymo Convent in Belem. San Jeronymo is the Patron Saint of Lisbon, and watches continually over its safety—preserving it from fires, earthquakes, inundations and such calamities. His zeal and vigilance of late years admit here of no question; although it is confessed that in 1755 he slumbered on his post, and did not awake until his statue was pitched from its pedestal prone upon its face. He was also, it cannot be denied, a little remiss in permitting the entrance of Junôt and his band of marauders; although it is averred that he did all in his power to remedy the evil by procuring favourable winds to waft Sir Arthur here to drive them out. On the whole, San Jeronymo is a respectable Patron Saint—much revered in Lisbon; and who, since his canonization, has done as much good as any saint in the calendar.

About this time I witnessed the grand Lisbon hoax of the cork-boots. The wag was a British artillery officer, who managed to bring half the city to Belem, to see a man walking on the water across the river. It was a humbug on the largest scale; for, I suppose there could not be less than thirty thousand people present, by land and water. The matter was managed remarkably well; and such was the implicit confidence of the multitude that a lane was made by the police for the performer, from the house where he resided to the Belem steps, to keep off the pressure of the crowd. The thing passed off good-naturedly; and when the joke became known the immense mass melted away insensibly, and without any disturbance.

In the month of December I was appointed assistant-surgeon to the 66th regiment,[1] and directed once more to proceed to Coimbra.

---

1. In consequence of the severe loss this excellent corps sustained on the bloody field of Albuera, it was formed into a provisional battalion, with two or three other weak corps, and laboured under this disadvantage during the remainder of the Peninsular struggle—though only joined in battalion, for the greater part of the time, with the 31st regiment. The 66th, for its strength, was one of the most efficient corps in the army—it always fought well—was well-behaved and on good terms with the inhabitants in quarters, and had few sick. A high compliment was paid to this regiment, by the Duke of Wellington, during a sharp little affair un the advance from Coimbra to Oporto, in 1809. In riding past Capt. Goldie, (later Colonel Goldie, of the 11th Foot,) then commanding two companies, the Duke stopped and halted there, saying, "You may take your men back, and tell your commanding officer, they have fought like lions today."

CHAPTER 11

Siege and Storm of Badajoz

What rein can hold licentious wickedness,
When down the hill he holds his fierce career?
We may as bootless spend our vain commands
Upon the enraged soldiers in their spoil,
As send precepts to the Leviathan
To come ashore——

　　　　　　　　　　　Shakespeare.

Mounted on my bay horse, Liberdade, with my baggage on a mule in charge of Antonio, I set out from Lisbon, on the 23rd January, 1812. An agreeable brother-*medico* travelled in company.

Our first day's march was a short one of two leagues to Saccavem: next day we passed through Alhandra and saw the eastern extremity of the far-famed lines of Torres Vedras. We admired (as who does not) the foresight and sagacity, that had appreciated the strength and value of these mountain bulwarks, and the skill and secrecy with which they had been rendered impregnable.

We met with few incidents of importance on our march. At Azimbuzia my horse thought proper to break out of his stable, and run away amongst a drove of his brethren, who were grazing on the extensive flats near that village. It took us three hours to catch him. At Santarem, the blood of the French general, St. Croix, (I think,) who was killed by a shot from our gunboats on the Tagus, was yet to be seen on the wall.

We witnessed a great deal of misery amongst the poor inhabitants on this march, who were slowly returning to their burnt and dilapidated homes, with exhausted means and worn-down and emaciated frames—everyone having his peculiar tale of distress to tell, but all were unanimous in their exclamations of bitter hatred to the *"malditos Franceses."* The cutting down of the olive trees for fuel was one charge constantly reiterated against Massena's troops. The poor people said they did not mind so much the burning and breaking up of their furniture, or even making bonfires of their houses, as the wanton destruction of the trees from which their revenue was mainly derived, and which took so long a time to arrive at maturity.

Between Thomar and Espinhal my companion and myself, after a long wet march, were benighted in a wretched condition of cold and hunger, still two leagues from our destination. A light being observed a little way from the road, we turned our horses' heads up a lane that led to it, and threw ourselves on the hospitality of the owner of a large house which we soon reached. The *fidalgo* appeared a very civil and hospitable person, and received us with great cordiality and kindness. A huge fire was kindled forthwith—our clothes were dried, and a couple of hares and a leash of partridges put down to roast. In a little more than an hour we sat down to a good supper—our jaded animals having been also well fed. After supper our kind host put a kettle of *vin du pays*, with sugar and spice, on the blazing logs, with which we regaled ourselves till a late period of the night, the *fidalgo* telling us the wonders of Rio de Janeiro which he had heard from his daughter, who was maid of honour to the Queen, and had accompanied the Royal Family on their emigration to Brazil.

In the morning the excellent *fidalgo* appeared a little too desirous of receiving some compensation for his hospitality. He took a fancy to my mule—a strong animal worth a hundred dollars, and offered one in exchange not worth fifty. But Antonio, who was the channel of the proposal, said he durst not speak to me on the subject, as the mule was a favourite and had been foaled in the family.

When we reached Coimbra, Ciudad Rodrigo had fallen, and troops and artillery were moving to the south, where preparations were making for investing Badajoz. The regiment to which I now belonged, I found, was quartered in Spanish Estremadura, somewhere near Merida. Important events being expected in that neighbourhood, I was directed to proceed without delay to join it.

As I was sitting at breakfast the morning before leaving Coimbra, Major C——, commanding a regiment of Portuguese *Caçadores*, rushed into the room in a state of great agitation, enquiring for a surgeon. I went with him immediately. The regiment was drawn up in line on parade—there was a group of officers a little in front surrounding a soldier who was moaning, apparently in great pain. I found that in dressing the line the major had, unthinkingly, used the point instead of the flat of his sword; and the wounded man, either from stumbling, or that strange fascination that is believed to throw the bird into the jaws of the snake—had pressed against it and given himself a mortal stab. The wound was so small as to be scarcely visible, and there was no bleeding. He died the same evening.

I retraced my steps to Thomar—crossed the picturesque Zezere at Punhete, and proceeded from thence to Abrantes along the right bank of the Tagus, which here is literally golden-sanded—to appearance. It is, I believe, only the mica which has been washed out of the granite during the long course of the stream, nearly all the way from Toledo.

Halting for a couple of days at Abrantes, which was a large depot of sick, I had the pleasure of meeting many old acquaintances, and of visiting all the hospitals. This is a very convenient station for sick on many accounts—chiefly the healthy character of the place and the direct water communication with Lisbon.

Proceeding on our march, the faithful Antonio and I crossed into the Alentejo—had a shot at a wolf without hitting him, near Gaviao, and reached Elvas on the 20th March. At this time the last siege of Badajoz was just commencing—Lord Wellington's headquarters were at Elvas—the town was full of staff, and all was bustle and note of preparation. The weather was very wet, and I pitied the poor fellows up to their middles in the trenches. The Guadiana was very much swollen, and fears were entertained that the bridges would be carried away and the siege raised. Elvas is only three leagues from Badajoz, and from the top of my house I could see very distinctly with a glass the operations that were going on.

At Elvas I learned that the 66th was quartered at Merida—the direct road would be through Badajoz, but as that route was not then practicable, I was ordered to march by the circuitous line of Campo Mayor and Albuquerque.

We entered Spain at the latter town, and the change was striking and agreeable. The houses were cleaner and better furnished, and a glass window would be seen occasionally. The people were better dressed, and the women infinitely superior. But everybody knows that the sweet *Espagnolas* are very fascinating, and five hundred descriptions have made all the world acquainted with their merits, so that I can only corroborate what has already been often and much better said on the subject—and add that they skim over the ground so serially, and wear the *basquina* and *mantilla* so gracefully, and their Cinderella shoes so daintily, and manoeuvre their fans so *coquettishly*—and have such magnificent eyes and lovely shapes—and talk so endearingly, and lisp so prettily, and smile so affectionately, and waltz so charmingly, that I wonder I brought away the bigness of a hazelnut of heart untouched out of the country.

When we arrived at Albuquerque the cannonading at Badajoz had begun, and the next morning, the weather being fine, all the world was out on the walls of the castle (situated on a high hill) to witness the exciting spectacle. Although twenty miles distant, every shot could be heard distinctly; and at first, before a broad pall of smoke covered besiegers and besieged, everything going on could be seen with a glass. When I mounted to the castle, after breakfast, I found a great crowd of well dressed spectators with many ladies. Deep interest was painted on every countenance; and no wonder, for many of those now assembled were inhabitants of Badajoz, and had obtained permission from Phillippon, the French Governor, to quit the city when it was first invested; leaving their homes, and some their husbands and families, behind. Every shot they now heard might be pregnant with the fate of some dear relative.

Yet, though concern and apprehension were manifest in the countenance, there was nothing unmanly in the demeanour of the male part of the assembled crowd, nor any silly expression of violent emotion on the part of the ladies. Their whole conduct, as well as that of the men, produced an impression on my mind favourable to the Spanish character. As the visitation that might in a moment cut off their dearest connexions, and render them homeless and destitute, was inevitable; and as the capture of the place was for the ultimate benefit of the country, they appeared to acquiesce in the sad necessity of the siege without a murmur—only hoping it would soon be over.

There was one singularly fine and handsome woman, Donna Thereza Solvielta, and two sweet girls her daughters, whom I particularly observed, as they happened to be ascending the castle hill at the same time with myself. When they took their position at the top and directed their eyes towards the beleaguered city, I observed that every shot, as the sound boomed sullenly on the ear, paled the lovely cheeks of the two young ladies, but the mother stood the fire better. At the first report there was a faint exclamation—"*O Virgem purissima!*" from one of the daughters; but they all soon became composed, and as I was beginning to feel an interest in the group, and my uniform as a British officer was a sufficient introduction, I accosted Donna Thereza, and thus commenced a most agreeable acquaintance with a very amiable family. When I informed them that in all probability no bombs would be thrown into the town, and that the English fire would be entirely directed against the ramparts and defences of the place, and thus that there was scarcely any danger of their house being hit, which was in the square near the cathedral—they were much consoled, for they had feared a general bombardment. It appeared that the husband and two boys remained in Badajoz. After listening and reconnoitring through a glass until we were tired, I walked about with the ladies until the sun became hot, and then escorted them home to their lodgings in the house of an old female relative.

The rain that fell lately had swollen the rivers crossing the road to Merida so much that they were unfordable, and the bridges had fallen in the wars—I was thus detained three days at Albuquerque. The morning was spent on the hill, listening to the firing, and speculating about the siege with my new friends the Solvielta family. At length I bade those interesting ladies *adieu*, and Antonio and myself set out for Merida.

The cannonading sounded in our ears the whole way. We found more difficulty than we had expected in fording the rivers, and I very nearly lost my fine mule and all my baggage in crossing one of them. My trusty *criado* behaved remarkably well on this occasion, and shewed great firmness and presence of mind in keeping the animal's head against the stream when nearly carried away himself. I could be of little service, as I sat with my knees on the saddle and my feet on the horse's rump. After three or four unpleasant passages of this description we reached Merida, where I joined my regiment, commanded by a gallant soldier, Major Dodgin, and was formally introduced to the officers.

Merida is on the right bank of the Guadiana, forty miles above Badajoz. It is a very ancient city—was the seat of a Provincial Military Government under the Romans, and is still full of fine Roman remains. There is a long and beautiful bridge over the Guadiana, of the time of Charles the Fifth, but on a Roman foundation—a Roman and a Moorish aqueduct—a large piece of an amphitheatre—the remains of a *Naumachia*, a *Presidium* in a very perfect state of preservation, with several busts of Roman Emperors in the niches, amongst which I discovered the heads of Trajan and Galba—a triumphal arch—the *portico* of a Temple of Mars with "*Marti D. O. M*" on the base of the pediment. This *portico* is quite perfect: it stands in front of a Church of Dominican Friars, and immediately under the old inscription is the following:—"*Jam non Marti sed Jesu Christo, D. O. M., consecratum est.*"

This must be a fine field for an antiquarian. Although possessing small pretensions to black letter lore, I could not help feeling strong emotions in roaming about the vestiges of ancient grandeur and magnificence. The amphitheatre has been used not long ago as an arena for bull-fights—a small improvement on the bloody spectacles formerly exhibited, but still most barbarous, and evincing the little improvement that fifteen or sixteen centuries of a corrupted Christianity have produced on the national morals.

In the course of a day's rambles through the town I descried a handsome white marble *façade* of a Temple of Diana, built into the front of a modern house, which, from certain indications, afforded by the conduct of two or three young damsels at the windows, was unquestionably more devoted to the worship of Venus Urania than that of the chaste goddess. Here, at any rate, Paganism might triumph on the superior purity of its morals.

But on this occasion I had little time for antiquarian explorations—Soult, at this time, was collecting what force he could to relieve Badajoz, now hard pressed—which the covering array, under Sir Rowland Hill, was determined to prevent—consequently a fight was expected, and it became necessary to clear the hospitals and send all incumbrances to the rear. The sick of the second division, therefore, were ordered to Altar de Chao, an hospital station in the Alen-Tejo; and although I had only just arrived, after a march of five hundred miles, I was directed to take charge of the convoy.

The siege of Badajoz was still going on, and this march, as well as that by Albuquerque, were of high interest, from the vicinity of the route to the invested city. Our road now described a segment of a circle round it, within the former course and much nearer, and its lofty citadel was visible from every elevation of the way, standing above a heavy canopy of smoke which overhung the ramparts and lower parts of the town, as well as the besieging batteries. Generally, about three o'clock in the afternoon, there was a suspension of firing on both sides for a short time, to allow the guns to cool. Then the smoke would be wafted away by the wind, and the whole fortress become distinctly visible. Soon a salvo would thunder from the breaching batteries, and be immediately answered by the garrison, and then the incessant roar of the heavy artillery on both sides would proceed without intermission as before.

During all this time the weather was remarkably fine and clear, as if the elements wished now to atone for their unkind treatment of the allied troops at the commencement of the siege. I reached Campo Mayor on the 6th of April, with my convoy of sick, and was much pleased to find that the poor fellows had all improved wonderfully in health during the march. Indeed, the good effects of locomotion in recovering very debilitated subjects, were strikingly displayed during the whole Peninsular struggle, but never more than on this occasion. The convoy consisted of one hundred and twenty sick, thirty or forty of whom were so ill of bad continued and remittent fevers, that it was necessary to tie them on the mules' backs, lest they should fall off through weakness.

Others were supported by men of the escort sitting behind them; but at the end of the second day's march these enfeebled subjects would ride by themselves bravely and vigorously, and call out lustily for their rations. I am convinced that the lives of several amongst them were saved by this march, and the recovery of the rest was materially accelerated. To be sure ours was a march cheered by the most exciting military music all the way; and the sound of the twenty-four pounder salvos, with the occasional glimpse of the smoke-wreathed city, and the French flag still flying on the citadel, formed a cordial more tonic and stimulating and restorative than all the elixirs in the world.

On the 6th of April, the last day of our march, the cannonade was much louder and closer than usual, and as I rode along I became more and more convinced that a crisis was approaching. On our arrival in the evening, at Campo Mayor, we found the whole population in a state of intense excitement and anxiety. It was generally known that Badajoz was to be stormed during the night; and as we were only seven miles distant, even the pattering of the musketry could be distinctly heard in the calm of the evening, between the heavy reports of the battering artillery. As the night advanced every accidental swelling of the sound was deemed the signal for the terrific conflict at the breach. I know not how the intelligence was received, but most certainly there were reports in circulation that night, at Campo Mayor, that the castle was to be escaladed by Sir Thomas Picton and the third division.

During this eventful night few eyes were closed in Campo Mayor: the priests were performing divine service and imploring success in the churches, and the entire adult population were either engaged in prayer, or traversing the streets, in extreme agitation and alarm. All this time the thunder of the bloody conflict sounded awfully, and as the work of death advanced, and the air became cooler and stiller, the report of the heavy artillery appeared actually to shake the roofs of the churches over the trembling masses crowded within. The scene altogether was one that cannot easily pass from the memory, for it was marked by astonishing sublimity. I hurried from one church to another; but all were alike—all were filled with people praying with extreme fervency—weeping, sobbing, exclaiming—enquiring wildly and anxiously for intelligence, or listening intently to the loud and confused sound of mortal strife.

At length day dawned, and with it came an ominous calm and lull. Did this bode good or evil? Was the city taken, or had the storming parties been shattered and repulsed, and had the garrison ceased its fire because the besiegers had retired from the reach of the guns? People asking these questions and circulating the thousand rumours that had been created on the instant, looked anxiously into each other's faces, pale and shrunk with fear and suspense and the harassing vigils of the night. As it became clearer the greater part left the churches and streets and repaired to the ramparts, straining all eyes in the direction of Badajoz. For a long time nothing could be descried on the wide plain between the two places—at length a horseman was seen galloping full speed along the road. The agony of suspense then became almost intolerable: but when he approached nearer and was seen to stop suddenly, stand up in his stirrups and wave his hat repeatedly round his head—a shout of ten thousand "*Vivas!*" rent the air, prolonged and reiterated along the fortifications, until lost in the overwhelming pealing of all the bells in the city.

My military dress procured me two or three score of warm embraces—the pale countenances of the women brightened up and their dark eyes beamed out brilliantly. Never were fair ladies so condescending and so affectionate, and I believe, if I had chosen, I might have kissed half Campo Mayor. "*Viva os Inglezez!*" was in every mouth. At length getting satiated with the numerous accolades, and remembering that my day's march was a short one, I delayed the starting of my sick convoy for a couple of hours, and determined to gallop over to Badajoz.

I reached the bridge over the Guadiana in three quarters of an hour, but my surprise was great; Instead of finding everything quiet, and everybody occupied in attentions to the wounded and preparations for burying the dead, as I had expected, I beheld a scene of the most dreadful drunkenness, violence and confusion. Parties of intoxicated men, loosed from all discipline and restraint, and impelled by their own evil passions, were roaming and reeling about; firing into the windows—bursting open the doors by the discharge of several muskets simultaneously against the lock—plundering—shooting any person who opposed them—violating, and committing every horrid excess, and sometimes destroying each other. There were many Portuguese, but the majority were English soldiers; and amongst these, two regiments of the third division, the eighty ——— and ——— were disgracefully conspicuous.

I proceeded amidst a desultory but dangerous firing, by the *detour* of the Talavera gate to the main breach. There, indeed, was a most awful scene, where

———*Mars might quake to tread.*

There lay a frightful heap of fifteen hundred British soldiers, dead, but yet warm, and mingled with some still living, but so desperately wounded as to be irremovable without more assistance than could yet be afforded—there they lay stiffening in their gore—body piled upon body—involved, intertwined, crushed, burned and blackened—one hideous and enormous mass of carnage, whilst the slanting morning sunbeams, feebly irradiating this hill of slain, appeared to my imagination, pale and lugubrious as during an eclipse.

At the foot of the castle wall, where the third division had escaladed, the dead lay thick, and a great number of corpses were strewn near the Vincente Bastion. Several were scattered on the glacis of the Trinidad Bastion, and a number who appeared to have been drowned, were lying in the cunette of the ditch, at that place. But the chief slaughter had taken place at the great breach. There stood still the terrific beam across the top, armed with its thickly bristling sword-blades, which no human strength nor dexterity could pass without impalement. The smell of burned flesh was yet shockingly strong and disgusting.

Joining some of the medical officers who were assisting the most urgent cases, and amputating limbs shattered by round-shot, I remained during the morning and forenoon; then, hastily eating a biscuit, partially blackened with gunpowder, and taking a mouthful of wine from a soldier's wooden canteen, I returned to my charge at Campo Mayor. The bells were still ringing merrily at intervals, and everybody was rejoicing—rejoicing! after what I had just witnessed!

After the terrific sacrifice of two thousand of the very best and bravest troops in the world! After the blood-compacted pile still fresh in my eye! After the piteous meanings and dying ejaculations yet torturing my hearing! Rejoicing after all this!

I hastened to get my party in motion, and with many bitter reflections on the calamities of war, proceeded on the march. I am not ashamed to acknowledge—for it was a natural feeling to inexperienced and unsophisticated youth—that I felt low-spirited and unhappy during the remainder of the march to Altar de Chao. When I arrived there I had an attack of low fever, which was fortunately of short duration, and in a few days my trusty Antonio and his master retraced their steps towards Estremadura.

When we had advanced about a league on our first day's march towards Elvas, we saw at a distance a large body of men approaching. It was the French garrison of Badajoz, about three thousand five hundred in number, on their route to embark for England. As, I suppose, would be the case with any other troops under similar circumstances, there was a striking difference in the appearance and bearing of the veterans from that of the young soldiers. The former had a bold and self-confident look, that said, "*N'importe—c'est la fortune de guerre—notre temps viendra*" The poor young conscripts, of whom there appeared a fourth-part, on the contrary, looked completely *abuttus*; and their furtive, timid glances, betrayed the fear of discovering a loaded gun or a Portuguese knife in every object around them.

On our return through Elvas, the town was full of wounded; yet, in passing through the hospitals one would form a very incorrect opinion of the miseries and agonies that followed the storm, from the appearance of the patients. To have been wounded and to have escaped with life from such a tremendous conflict—involving a display of the most sustained, unflinching and perfect valour, in the course of many ages—was, in itself alone, a cause of pride and gratulation. I never witnessed such cheerfulness in suffering, as amongst these fine fellows; and there was something of moral interest that obtruded itself on the mind in observing their manly bearing, and the kindness and sympathy evinced towards each other. These brave men had dared the dangers and undergone the fatigues of the trenches and the batteries—the siege and the storm; and the warmest admiration of their noble conduct through all could be felt without any admixture of a neutralising feeling. *They* were untainted with the pillage of the devoted city, and the thousand atrocious crimes comprised in that fatal word.

At this time there was a strong muster of medical officers in Elvas, and the hospitals afforded a fine field of practice and great professional facilities in acquiring surgical confidence and experience. I obtained permission to stay there a fortnight.

On our return through Badajoz, I entered that ill-fated place with very painful feelings. All was still gloom and dismay: it was noonday and not time for the *siesta* yet, though not a soul was to be seen in the streets. No reaction had yet taken place after the horrors of the storm, and people, by a kind of tacit understanding, agreed to be silent as to the past, for it was too dreadful to contemplate. Almost every individual of any respectability in the city had been outraged, either in his property or the sanctity of his family, relations or friends. Happy were the ladies that had left the town before its investment. Those beautiful Solvieltas—had they remained! and from my heart I rejoiced at their escape.

Although the British and Portuguese troops—but chiefly the former—bore then, and still bear the principal share of the odium, the lower classes of the inhabitants were also chief performers in the horrid tragedy. The rascally mob—the disgrace of all large cities—as soon as the magazine of brandy in the cathedral was opened, joined, when they became half-drunk, in all the brutalities of the time. Having superior local knowledge, they conducted the English and Portuguese strangers to the houses of the principal and richest inhabitants, and when the doors were burst open, shared in the spoil and the crime.

Yet, originally, the blame lay with the Spaniards themselves, and even during the storm they provoked the wrath of the assailants. Had not Mendizabal behaved like a coward or a fool, Badajoz would never have fallen into the power of the French. When covering the place in an almost unassailable position, under San Christoval, defended by two rivers, a fortress and a fort, he suffered himself to be surprised by Soult, with half his force, and himself and his army to be driven from their strong post and scattered all over the country. And this route was the more shameful, as he had been previously warned by Lord Wellington and advised to be on his guard against Soult, but with true Spanish pride and mulishness scorned the good advice, and affected to believe that the French general would not dare to attack him.

Again, even after the dispersal of Mendizabal's army, had the Governor held out three days longer—assured as he was of speedy succour after the retreat of Massena from Santarem, and which was on its way to join Lim—the town could not have been taken by the French. But the truth is, the magniloquent Spaniards, to use a vulgar expression, scarcely ever shewed any pluck.

I believe it is true that the troops of the fourth division, who got into the town by escalading the San Vincento Bastion, when straggling through the deserted but illuminated streets, were fired upon out of the houses by the Spaniards. It is natural that this would be mentioned to their comrades, and, when the whole allied force burst into the city, be a pretext, if not an extenuation, for many of the excesses that were committed.

On the 22nd of April, I rejoined my regiment at Almandralejo, a considerable town, situated in a fertile plain, at that time covered with wheat. Sir Rowland Hill's headquarters were there established.

CHAPTER 12

Badajoz

A phlebotomia auspicandum esse curationem non a pharmacia.
Heinsius.

In the beginning of May, the cavalry picquets of our division post-ed near Hornachos, being considered a little too much exposed, the light companies of General Byng's brigade were sent to a small village called Puebla del Prior, to support them. I was directed to accompany the detachment.

This village was situated on a rising ground, rather uncomfortably close to the enemy's *videttes*. One day a brother officer and myself rode to Hornachos, a town two leagues farther in front, which was occasionally patrolled by both armies. It was a silly excursion, for we might both have been shot or taken prisoners; and as it was we were chased by two of the enemy's dragoons, but being better mounted and in lighter riding order, we soon found we could distance our pursuers if we chose; we consequently checked our horses and tried to inveigle them into an ambuscade. But they were old hands, and when they found how matters stood, they deliberately turned and went back to their patrol without even wasting a cartridge on us.

After passing a fortnight quietly at Puebla, we were disturbed one day whilst at dinner, by the approach of a strong body of the enemy's cavalry, before whom our advanced picquets were slowly retiring. The French came on slowly so as to give my faithful valet time to pack his baggage, place it on *Mulo* and retire, whilst the garrison prepared to defend the post. They came close, but did not attack as they had no infantry; and it afterwards appeared that this little demonstration was a mere reconnaissance to feel our force—Sir Rowland having at this time marched to destroy the French *tête du pont* and forts at Almaraz on the Tagus.

When Sir Rowland Hill returned, after the successful accomplishment of his object, with little loss, we advanced in the direction of Zafra and the Sierra Morena. At Usagre, we had the mortification of witnessing the defeat of two brigades of British heavy cavalry, by about an equal number of French, from the top of the church tower. This sight caused great disgust, as from the superior physical strength of our men and horses they ought to have been more than a match for their adversaries. The French were commanded by General L'Allemand, and the British by General S——, who was much blamed at the time for absolute deficiency of personal intrepidity in leading on his men. In the evening the wounded began to arrive at the village, and I sat up all night dressing their hurts—mostly sabre-cuts.

Soon after this, a large French corps having collected in our front, Sir Rowland Hill's corps retired to the celebrated position of Albuera, and commenced fortifying the fighting ground by field-works. The dry grass, luxuriant after the slaughter of the year before, was set fire to, to clear the front of the redoubts, and prevent a repetition of the calamities of Talavera, where the wounded on both sides suffered so dreadfully from the accidental conflagration. On this occasion, it was almost painful to see hares, and partridges, and game of various kinds, with which the country abounded, straying about, disconsolate for this premature destruction of their young.

In the end of June, my commanding officer, Major Dodgin, was attacked with a violent inflammatory fever, and I received orders to convey him to Badajoz and attend him there. Notwithstanding extensive depletion from the temporal arteries, and other measures necessary to subdue ardent fever in a patient of very large and robust frame—strong as a horse and weighing twenty stone—he became violently delirious. Under the hallucination that he had been appointed *aide-de-camp* to Sir Rowland Hill, he insisted one morning on dressing himself, mounting his horse and proceeding back to camp. After fruitlessly attempting to reason him out of this project, I found I must employ stronger measures; accordingly, having first removed the major's sword, pistols and trowsers out of the way, and left him in charge of two servants, I proceeded to the general hospital in quest of more assistance and a straight-waistcoat.

Here I found a certain pragmatic staff-surgeon, named B——, whom I begged to afford me the necessary aid, and also to give me his personal help in subduing the Hercules with whom I had to do. Now, it so chanced that the staff-surgeon in question had attended General Walker, who was so badly wounded at the storm. The patient had had several ribs broken, but recovered; and his doctor being a good draughtsman, had made a sketch of this remarkable wound, and was, unfortunately, when I called, engaged in giving it the finishing touch. I waited a few minutes, but seeing him still intent on his work, I then requested that he would leave off his sketch and accompany me to my refractory patient's lodging, or he might get away, and in the powerful sun that was then broiling us, soon ride himself to death. "My dear Sir," he replied, "just wait one instant; it will not take more than one moment. Look there, what do you think of that? Is the colouring too high? I had much difficulty in managing that flesh—hah, hah! *both* ways—hah, hah, hah! Doesn't that rib *relievo* a *leetle* too much—Eh? Certainly it does—don't you think so? I'll just soften it down a little." At last, after a quarter of an hour's shading down General Walker's too prominent rib, out we sallied with two orderlies and a straight-waistcoat.

Now, I had anticipated mischief from the delay, and was not mistaken. When we came to the top of the short street where the major lodged, we were both horror-struck at seeing him dressed in his blue frock and cocked-hat, leading his large black charger out of the door and preparing to mount. We all ran down the street as fast as we could, but he was on horseback before we reached his quarter. The staff-surgeon then accosted him, representing very eloquently that the major was not in a condition for a journey in the hot sun—that he would fall from his horse on the road, &c. &c. The major told him to begone—that he was a meddling fool or a madman thus to interrupt him when ordered on duty—and then finding his opponent still resolute, he set spurs to his horse and charged the poor doctor. The latter jumped to one side in great alarm and disappeared through a low window, that was fortunately open.

The patient then proceeded in a canter down the street towards the ramparts, and afterwards turned to the right in the direction of the Elvas gate, but I ran by a near cut and arrived there before him. I found some difficulty in explaining to the Spanish lieutenant, who commanded the guard, the nature of the case; but at length he did as I wished, and when the major arrived, looking very pale, the gate was closed and there was no egress. He fumed, and fretted, and threatened the officer—but it was all in vain; then turning his horse he galloped towards the Talavera gate, taking the same circuitous course by the ramparts. There, also, he was anticipated, for whilst I ran to the one, I had sent a servant to the other. A good deal fatigued by all this exertion in a burning sun, and weakened by loss of blood, the patient rode home, lay down on a couch and called for his writing desk. He then began a letter of charges against me for forcibly detaining him in Badajoz, but not being able to finish it, and soon writing diagonally instead of across the paper, he gave over, lay down and fell fast asleep. He slept nearly thirty-six hours, when he awoke convalescent—free from all complaint but weakness, and recollecting nothing that had happened.

It appeared that when I went to the hospital he started out of bed, soon mastered all opposition, and proceeded to dress himself. He was very angry at the removal of his sword and trowsers, and I had imagined that the absence of the latter would be an impediment to escape not easily got over—but I was wrong. The major made one of the servants surrender the trowsers he had on, banging him with a stick until he took them off, and such was his strength and determination that he fairly cowed them both into submission. The man's trowsers were too small, but he forced them on, though at the expense of some fearful rents in the thighs, and, indeed, the major might as well have been altogether *sans culottes*, as invested with the tattered concerns. He then went to the stable, saddled his horse himself, and actually brought him into his bedroom, which was on the ground-floor, until he found his cocked-hat. Had we been one minute later, or failed in blockading him at the gates, the poor patient would, in all probability, have ridden till he dropped dead from his horse.

After this adventure the major soon recovered and proceeded to join the regiment, but without his surgeon. It was the month of August, when the banks of the Guadiana are annually afflicted with bad remittent and intermittent fevers—I caught the disease, struggled against it for a little, but at last was obliged to surrender at discretion.

I had no particular desire to employ the facetious rib-painter, so I confided myself to the charge of a young *medico*, a friend and countryman, who watched me with the most kind and sedulous attention. From a desire to save the vital fluid and economize strength, he would not bleed me from the arm or temporal artery, as I wished; but when the symptoms of determination to the head became urgent, he sheered and shaved my curly locks one hot afternoon, and attached three dozen of leeches to my poor caput. A few hours after, they carried me into the yard, placed me erect, and poured four or five-and-twenty buckets of cold well-water over me from a third story window. After this terrible shower-bath, I was rubbed dry and put to bed. For the first two hours I was not quite sure whether my head had not been carried away in the flood, for I felt as if there was no living part, and all was numb and cold above my shoulders—but there was violent reaction during the night, and I became delirious the next morning.

However, I was not destined to leave my bones in Badajoz—there were but too many British bones there already. By the blessing of Providence, which, laughter-loving mortal that I am, I am not ashamed to acknowledge—I at length recovered, but, in the dreadfully hot weather we then had in Estremadura, the convalescence was tedious.

Throughout the Peninsular campaigns, many officers have complained that they never had the good luck to meet with civil treatment in their billets—a few others have been more lucky in having uniformly come in contact with good "*patrones*" occupying respectable houses, and possessing both the means and the inclination for the exercise of attention and hospitality. I belong to the latter fortunate class. On this occasion, when I so much required the aid of the social charities, I was as lucky in a good *patrone*, as on landing in Lisbon. I lodged in the house of a kind-hearted young priest, Don Juan Joze Martinez, who had two sisters living with him, and a third, the abbess of a convent in the same street. The young *senhoras* were exceedingly kind and attentive; perhaps the more so, when they discovered from my servant that I was an Irishman, which, in Spain, is synonymous with Roman Catholic.

However, to do these good ladies justice, although they were undeceived in this respect, they did not relax the least in those thousand little affectionate acts which my helpless situation called for, and those soothing offices of female kindness, so delightful to the object, when on a bed of sickness in a strange land. But they were very urgent in their endeavours to convert me from my heresy and bring me within the pale of their own church, seasoning each cup of the nice broth they prepared and administered with good advice on this subject, and often calling in their brother to their assistance. He was stronger-minded and more liberal, however, than these dark-eyed maidens, and used to reply to their entreaties, "*Deixa lo, deixa lo, Pobrecito*"—"Let him alone, poor fellow—we must cure him first and convert him afterwards."

When I became convalescent, a strange Spanish gentleman called to see me. He said he had been requested by his wife and daughters to enquire concerning my health, and to express on their parts grateful thanks for the attentions they had received at Albuquerque. It was Don Ignacio Solvielta, and as soon as I recovered sufficiently I called on my fair friends. It was pleasing to learn that their house had remained untouched during the siege; and in the sack and pillage of the storm, although the door had been blown open, a bag of a couple of hundred dollars was the amount of their loss. I felt pure and lively joy at their exemption from the general misery that bowed down the unhappy city.

My *patrone* gave me a graphic description of the state of his family during the dreadful two days, which Badajoz was the prey of a drunken and infuriated soldiery. He had sagaciously anticipated the plunder, and provided two purses—a larger and a smaller—placed his sisters on the top of the house and then destroyed the ladder—after these precautions the doors were secured and the courageous priest quietly awaited the result. About eight o'clock, the first morning, a party of half-drunken British soldiers, in yellow facings, blew off the lock of the street door, rushed in and seized him, and demanded his money. He pleaded poverty, but they presented their muskets to his breast, and at last, by horrid threats, extorted the smaller purse. They then searched the house, destroying or pillaging whatever struck their fancy; at length they went away and the door was barricaded as well as circumstances permitted.

In the course of the first day another party—also British and with the same facings, broke through the poor priest's defences—roamed through the house, and afterwards by threats of instant death, forced him to surrender the larger purse of dollars. The door was then left open, but the house was no more molested. The poor trembling girls regained all that day and night on the roof, and did not venture down till some degree of order was restored in the town.

During the siege two twenty-four pound shot had penetrated the back wall of the house and lodged in the front, without doing farther injury than piercing a wooden partition and demolishing an armchair, from which one of the sisters had just risen. The priest intended to keep them both, though, as he remarked, they were not in the habit in his church of preserving relics so substantial.

A veil was thrown purposely over the sufferings of his sister the Abbess, and the inmates of the convent, which was never withdrawn, for when I ventured to enquire if they had escaped insult and outrage, my *patrone's* brow grew black. It was then only I could fully appreciate the fine character of the man. Smarting under recent violence and spoliation, and, moreover touched, as there was too much reason to believe, in a point on which Spanish honour is so peculiarly susceptible, he yet had the good sense not to confound the innocent with the guilty, and the magnanimity still to treat me with the greatest tenderness when lying helpless under his roof.

At this time the heat of the weather was extraordinary in Estremadura—the Fahrenheit thermometer rising to 97 degrees in the shade at Badajoz. Under these circumstances it was not easy to recover strength fast; but, having heard that the army was about to move to the front, I became anxious to join, and marched ten days before I ought to have set out. The consequence was an attack of ague on the road; and though the temperature in the sun could not have been less than 130 degrees, my teeth danced and chattered for an hour or so, like a pair of *castanets*, and I was forced to halt in a village on the road, named Santa Martha.

At this time the army was six months in arrears of pay, and, consequently, a good deal of inconvenience was occasionally experienced from narrow finances, particularly when absent from one's regiment. Two or three days after my arrival in Santa Martha, when taking a farewell look at my last dollar, and devising some plan of ways and means suited to the emergency, a mounted soldier of the 66th arrived in the village, with a letter from Fuentes del Maestro, where the regiment was quartered. It was Colonel Nicol's servant with a very kind letter, giving me unlimited leave of absence, and accompanied by three *doubloons*, which he thought I might require; and which, it appeared afterwards—such was the scarcity of money—he had been obliged to borrow from a Turkish Sutler who accompanied the division.

I record this trait of my most esteemed friend, now General Nicol, (as at time of first publication), because, in the first place, it is gratifying to my own feelings; and, secondly, because it was one of a series of similar acts of thoughtful and unostentatious liberality and kindness towards his officers, during a quarter of a century that he commanded the regiment.

At length I rejoined the 66th at Fuentes del Maestro, just in time to accompany it on the advance of the division in the direction of Llerena; but, on some intelligence being received of the concentration of a strong force of the enemy on our right, the division was countermarched, and our brigade, consisting of the Buffs or 3rd Foot, the 31st, 57th and 66th, returned to their old quarters at Fuentes del Maestro.

The day of our return was hot, and the road had been very dusty, with a good deal of wind. When the brigade reached the immediate neighbourhood of the town, they halted and piled their arms until the men were furnished with billets.

Near this spot was one of the old fountains from which the place had taken its name, which was a square enclosure, now in a ruinous state, and half filled with grass and weeds, but still containing clear water. The thirsty soldiers, fatigued with the heat and long inarch, flew at once to this reservoir, and kneeling and placing their hands on the low wall that surrounded it, they dipped their dusty muzzles up to the ears in the cool element and quaffed away like fishes.

The consequence was awful in the extreme.

Next morning about one hundred and fifty of them came to the different regimental hospitals, and at first their cases looked rather alarming, for they were all spitting blood. On examination it was ascertained that they had fished up three or four hundred leeches from the old fountain, which was full of these little wretches. These bloodsuckers had attached themselves in the mouth, nostrils, throat, gullet, and even the stomach; higher or lower, according to the vigour of their own adhesive powers, or the strength of suction of the drinkers. We had a bloody day at the hospitals, although no lives were lost, except the leeches, and very hard it was to eject them. Some were noosed with a silk ligature by the tail and torn off, though many were thus cut in two, leaving the head still sticking. Several were dislodged by a strong solution of salt, and tobacco was used to others. Powerful emetics were necessary to oust the knowing ones that had reached the citadel of the stomach. At last the enemy were finally beaten from all their positions with great slaughter.

The whole Corps of Sir Rowland Hill, consisting of sixteen or seventeen thousand men, was now set in motion towards the Sierra Morena, to dislodge the French from a rich tract of country to the west of those mountains which they had long occupied, co-operate with the forward movement of the main army under Lord Wellington in person, and push up the valley of the Tagus and even advance upon Madrid. We marched on the 27th of August, reached Llerena on the 29th, and Don Benito on the 6th of September. Don Benito is a large town, a short distance from the Guadiana, and close to the field of battle where the Spaniards, under Cuesta, had been defeated by the French, under Victor, with dreadful loss. This rencounter is known as the Battle of Medellin; and it is averred, that on the evening of the battle the arms of the French dragoons were so much swollen by their exertions in cutting up the Spanish infantry, that they could scarcely be pulled out of the sleeves of their jackets. The Spanish cavalry had fled, *comme d'ordinaire*, leaving the foot to their fate.

My friend and commanding officer, Colonel Nicol, and I, rode out one beautiful evening to the scene of action, intending to visit Medellin before we returned. The ground was still covered with the usual unpleasant, though interesting relics of the combat—broken bits of arms and accoutrements, shreds of uniforms—here and there a cap with a sabre-cut, or the crown stove in, and occasionally a human skeleton or that of a horse. The Colonel happened to ride a lazy old Spanish charger, called *El Medico*. When we came to a level piece of cantering ground extending a long way before us, I touched my horse with the spur, and looking behind and exclaiming, "Come along old *Medico!*" I galloped on; but my course was destined to be short. I had not proceeded fifty yards, when a brace of partridges whirred up directly under the horse's nose—the startled animal bolted to one side at right angles with the road, depositing me across a huge grenadier skull that nearly stove in three or four of my ribs. The colonel was with me in a moment, and supported my head until I recovered from the shock, which was far from agreeable. I then proceeded to set my ribs to rights—my friend caught my horse with some difficulty, and we soon resumed our ride.

The English had never been in Don Benito before, and thus we enjoyed the good effects of the first burst of patriotism, friendship and hospitality of the inhabitants, after the long and oppressive occupation of their town by the enemy. Nothing was seen or heard but patriotic songs—swearing to the Constitution before the ugly picture of Ferdinand the Seventh, "*Viva los Inglesez!*" and *fêting* and dancing. The people seemed to be all mad with joy. On the night of the 12th of September, when we were all busily engaged at a ball, the Marquis of Worcester arrived with despatches from Headquarters to Sir Rowland Hill; in half an hour the party was broken up, and early in the morning the corps was put in motion for Truxillo. I recollect well the terrible wetting we all got in a thunder-shower as we were leaving the town, and when the sun had nearly dried our clothes during the march, our lower integuments were again dipped mid-thigh deep in fording the Guadiana.

The angry elements pelted us pitilessly on every opportunity till we arrived at Truxillo; and then, after a poor muleteer who was sitting on his mule, singing, "*Viva Ferdinando!*" had been killed by the lightning, it cleared up and we had very fine weather.

A large depot of provisions, and stores, and an hospital, were established at Truxillo. To my great mortification, the medical officer who was to take charge of the hospital, fell sick; I was directed by the staff-surgeon of the division to take his place and remain in charge at Truxillo, whilst the 66th regiment, with the whole corps, moved on Madrid.

CHAPTER 13

March to Elvas

Cujus a vertice ac nigricantibus oculis
Tale quiddam spirat ac ab aurea Venere.

Auson

Truxillo, corrupted from *Turris Julü*, its ancient name, is a place of high antiquity, having been a Roman *Praesidium*, and the head quarters of a legion. In modern times it is known as the birth-place of Pizarro. The house in which he was born, is a large, uninhabited, half-ruined building, in the principal square. Indeed, half the town is in ruins: I occupied the palace of the Medina-Sidonia family as a general hospital: and it was almost melancholy to see the straw-beds of the sick spread on the floors of the most magnificent apartments, and to behold on all sides similar incongruities, or still greater—pigsties, even on the ground-floors of edifices connected with some of the greatest names in Spanish history, and everything hastening rapidly to decay. A condition of things but too emblematical of the state of the monarchy.

I lodged in the mansion of the Conde de Q——, a descendant of Pizarro; a little old man, who, in right of his ancestor, always wore a small gold key outside the flap of his right coat pocket, of which he was very proud. He was very grandiloquent, as most Spanish gentlemen are—formal, courteous and pedantic. When he found I understood Spanish he shewed me into his library, which was the best I met with in Spain. I found there several English works which I did not expect, translated into Spanish, and looking grotesque enough in their Castilian dress. Amongst these were *Robinson Crusoe*, *Pamela* and *Harvey's Meditations*—the florid and inflated style of the last being exactly conformable to the Spanish idiom.

My insignificant and unpretending volumes purport to be recollections of past scenes in life and the consequent reflections which the judgment, having attained to a certain small degree of ripeness by experience, may form thereon. I believe I might, with great propriety, have named the whole concern—"Confessions of early errors"—at least that appellation would best befit the present chapter.

The Conde de Q—— had two daughters unmarried—Donna Francesca and Donna Bernarda, with the latter of whom, who was the younger and the prettier, I soon found myself falling desperately in love. My time was fully occupied during the whole of the day, for I had two hundred sick, and a number of officers to attend, with only one incompetent Spanish Hospital-Mate to assist me; but the evenings were devoted to dancing—forfeits, blind man's buff, alternating with lessons in Don Quixotte, singing and the guitar.

It is customary in Spain to take one's chocolate in bed very early in the morning, and as I have generally found it good policy to conform to peculiar national customs wherever I have been, when innocent and not prejudicial to health, Antonio would sometimes bring it to me, fuming and fragrant, by daylight. But more frequently the fairy-footed Bernarda, accompanied by Francesca, would appear at my bed-side, bearing a little silver salver, on which was a small gilded cup of chocolate, so thick and rich that the little delicate parallelopiped of toast, its unvarying attendant, would stand upright in the middle. There would the lovely sisters remain

——*twin cherries on one stalk*

in all honest confidence, laughing, and joking, and lisping their beautiful language, till I had finished my chocolate—a matter which I was never in a hurry to accomplish.

Let no man of vain imagination, nor woman either, entertain for a moment, a thought prejudicial to the amiable couple, for no sweet brace of sisters on record, chaste as

————*the icicle*
That hangs from Dian's Temple————

could have uniformly comported themselves with greater propriety.

I remained three months at Truxillo, and were I not afraid of swelling out my book to inexpedient dimensions, I could detail numerous incidents, some comic and some tragic, but all amusing enough at the time, in which I was engaged. Many love passages also must be omitted—how I had a Spanish rival in my admiration of the fair Bernarda—how she confessed I need fear no supplanting in her heart—how I was threatened with the *cuchillo* if I persisted in my presumption—how I received an anonymous letter, warning me of a plot to assassinate me, when paying a night-visit to a sick officer—how, with the assistance of the trusty Antonio and two of my hospital orderlies, the plotters were discomfited and soundly drubbed—how I discovered my little rival amongst them, and how I treated him on that occasion, professionally and *secundem artem*, by administering myself a good stiff dose of bark, *with the stick inside*—how I triumphed, and, alas! how, in the midst of my rejoicing, I was suddenly ordered to break up the hospital establishment at Truxillo and proceed to Elvas.

Young men under the influence of strong passions have done, do, and will do silly things, I presume, to the end of the chapter. On leaving Truxillo, I was prevented by an accident from making a fatal mistake early in life, and thus shading irreparably its whole complexion afterwards.

It was arranged that my mistress should elope with me on a fixed day, and a priest was to be ready at a village six leagues off, to unite us the same evening. As there are no post-chaises nor other procurable vehicles in that part of Spain, and the ladies must travel on ass-back or mule-back, I had purchased a quiet female donkey to carry her fair load. As this whole matter was *sub silentio*, for we feared the opposition of the Conde, Antonio negotiated that the owner of the animal should bring it to the stable late on the evening preceding the intended escapade. At the time appointed, the donkey was grazing in a field with several others; and, just before the proprietor had caught her, a fight and general row took place amongst the *bourros*—the quiet animal selected for me received a kick in the *mêlée* from one of her he-relations, that lamed her effectually—no ass was forthcomings when required, and time pressed, for Soult was advancing and our army in full retreat from Burgos. No other suitable conveyance could be procured at a short notice, and thus our scheme failed, and the ignoble kick of an ass knocked the best concerted plan in the world to pieces.

What great events from trivial causes spring.

After bidding farewell to as lachrymose a pair of sisters (poor girls!) as ever wept in each other's arms, I conducted my sick to Elvas, accompanied by a good-natured little doctor of the Buffs, and a gigantic officer of the 71st, Ralph Dudgeon, somewhere near seven feet high, but every inch a good fellow. On the march the little boys and girls followed him as a prodigy, and everybody stared up at him as if looking at a steeple. The roads at this time were infested by numerous bands of robbers, formed chiefly of deserters; but we marched in battle array, and although we had one alarm in a thick cork-tree wood, the rascals were frightened at our imposing appearance, and made off on the approach of our little but compact column.

At Badajoz I failed not to call on the good priest, my former kind host, and was concerned to find that one of the amiable sisters was suffering from a Tertian fever. Having prescribed for her and left her a supply of good medicine, (invaluable in Spain,) we marched to Elvas.

CHAPTER 14

Escape from Robbers

Every bullet has its billet.
Proverb.

When we reached Elvas we found that the most alarming reports were in circulation as to the defeat and dispersion of the British army, and the approaching advance of the enemy in overwhelming force into Portugal. It was even feared that another retreat to the lines of Torres Vedras might be necessary. A general gloom pervaded the city. I was ordered to remain and do duty in one of the general hospitals until farther orders.

In the course of a few days these rumours ceased, for certain intelligence arrived, that after suffering considerable loss, both in the unsuccessful attacks on the Castle of Burgos, and during the retreat from that city, the army was once more established in its old frontier positions, covering Portugal. Sir Rowland Hill's Headquarters were at Coria, and General Byng's Brigade, in which was the 66th, was stationed at Moralejo, a small town in the neighbourhood. I was then directed to march to that place.

We crossed the Tagus at Alcantara, a fortified town (after a fashion) on the left bank, where the river runs deep and rapid between two high rocky banks. The bridge is a fine relic of Roman power and skill; and, until the main arch was blown up two years before, was in good preservation, with the marble slab, even, yet perfect as from the sculptor's hand, telling who were Consuls and in what year of Trajan's reign it was built. It certainly was a daring attempt to lay the foundation of the piers of the arches in such a deep and impetuous stream, particularly as anything like coffer-dams must have been quite out of the question. I doubt whether all the skill in Spain could do the same thing now.

The Engineers had constructed a rope-bridge over the broken arch, which, from its great elevation, elasticity and broad span, shook under the passenger rather unpleasantly. When Antonio and I crossed, the day was very windy, and the bridge more than usually tremulous and unsteady; and although we dismounted, I was not without apprehensions, as a sudden gust would sweep violently through the deep gulley in which the river ran boiling below, that the slender flooring under our feet might be blown from its moorings, and all upon it tumbled into the Tagus.

Lord Wellington having now placed his army in winter quarters, was on his way to Cadiz, to concert measures with his brother the Marquis Wellesley and the Cortes, for a more perfect control over the Spanish armies, and the improvement of their very defective organization. We met him and General Alava the morning we crossed the Tagus, on the road between Zarza Mayor and Alcantara. After they passed us an aide-de-camp rode back and made enquiries about the bridge. I advised the party to dismount, and Lord Wellington and General Alava to get out of the coach in which they travelled, assuring him that if the gale increased much their only safety would be in holding by the mules' tails. But he only laughed at my good advice, and the idea of the great Wellington clinging to the *Os Coccygis* of a mule!

The next day an event occurred on the march, by no means of a laughing nature. As we were moving quietly along a plain thickly covered with the cystus shrub—Antonio, my English *Bat-man*, and the baggage a little in the rear, a musket ball whistled suddenly by, somewhere between my face and the horse's head, which made us both prick up our ears. I looked round, and there, plain enough, was the puff of smoke, about fifty yards from the road, amidst the tall shrubs. Incontinently I galloped on towards a little elevation in the road, and by the most extraordinary good fortune, not two minutes after, descried the head of a small column of cavalry coming along, half a mile off. They belonged to Don Julian Sanchez, and had been specially ordered to destroy a band of brigands, supposed to be in the neighbourhood.

I told the officer in command what had occurred, and we all hastened to the place where the shot had been fired. The dragoons dashed into the cystus very gallantly, and soon came upon a body of a dozen robbers, who shewed fight bravely enough, but to no purpose. The country was open, for the slender shrub was no greater hindrance to the movements of cavalry than a field of wheat—and the disparity of force so great that none of them could escape. After a short but animated affair, of which we were near spectators, the whole band were killed or made prisoners. I saw three of the gang afterwards strangled at Coria.

In this piquant little business, one dragoon received an ugly wound in the arm, which I dressed on the spot. Two of the prisoners had received some bad sabre-cuts, which I also offered to dress, but their ferocious captors would not permit it.

It had rained heavily lately, and every stream was much swollen, presenting numerous obstacles in our way, which we generally had to ford—the bridges being "few and far between." Here again my portable goods and chattels were in imminent danger, and once more Antonio forced the passages in gallant style, assisted by an honest *Bat-man*, yclept Jonathan Wild, but no relative, that I ever heard, of the prince of burglars. At the end of a long dreary day's march from Zarza, we reached the miserable town of Moralejo.

Here General Byng's Brigade were resting after the fatigues and privations of the Burgos retreat, although the indifferent rations, muddy streets and wretched hovels of this village, afforded but slender facilities for recovering health and efficiency. However, our brigade had suffered little, comparatively—the men having been well taken care of and well fed on the retreat, whilst others were starving, under the watchful eye of the best brigadier, assisted by Mr. Edwards, one of the best commissaries, in the service.

A branch of the Allagon, a large tributary of the Tagus, ran through Moralejo, which I soon explored, and found it contained good dace and barbel that served to eke out the rations, and nothing else was here procurable. Antonio managed, however, to turn the tough, lean, ropy beef into something like soup, and thus the programme of dinners was fish—soup—*bouilli*—Sunday—fish, *bouilli*, soup—Monday, and so on through the week.

We remained but a short time in Moralejo, and then moved to Coria, and afterwards to a large straggling village called Ceclavin. Coria is a walled city containing nine or ten thousand inhabitants—the walls are of Moorish origin with several round towers, but all in a ruinous state. The hill on which the city is built rises precipitately from the former bed of the River Allagon, which is now dry—the course of the stream having been in some way turned from its ancient channel into another, half a mile distant, though the bridge still stands oddly enough over the old course, and the river has now to be crossed by a ferry. The local tradition is, that Saint Somebody, whose name I forget, to whom the cathedral is dedicated, foreseeing that in the course of time the church's foundation would be undermined by the river, miraculously changed its course one night, and in the morning the astonished inhabitants beheld the stream running in a new channel at a respectful distance. Certainly the *puissant* Saint left his miracle incomplete, for, beyond all question, he ought to have endowed the river with the power of carrying off the bridge on its back.

A canon of the cathedral in relating this story, told me confidentially—"The people believe the legend, and we don't wish to undeceive them—they are the more devout for their faith. Between you and me the river's course was changed by the earthquake of 1755."

During this winter amateur plays and various festivities were got up at Coria, which continued to be Sir R. Hill's Headquarters. A pack of fox-hounds came out from England for the worthy commander, and hunted once or twice a week, until they were broke up by a singularly unfortunate accident.

One very fine day there was a strong field—we found and had a splendid run of nearly two hours, with only a short check—everybody well up. At last Mr. Reynard, being hard pressed, made for his earth in a steep bank of the Allagon, but feeling somewhat flurried with the long chase, the animal, wise as he was, forgot his topographical marks, and, instead of descending to his hole obliquely, he went sheer down a perpendicular bank, one hundred and fifty feet high, and was followed by five couple and a half of the best of the dogs. They were all killed instantly, and Sir R. Hill, the huntsman and two or three of the leading horsemen had a narrow escape; for the bank was most treacherous, giving no indication of danger until almost too late.

The amateur plays were not much patronised by the Spaniards, and the necessary substitution of men for female performers revolted the ladies, who turned up their pretty noses at the want of grace and elegance of movement and dress. The masculine strides in petticoats upon the stage must have been an utter abomination in the eyes of those mincing beauties, whose longest step would not be more than three or four inches.

Here, as everywhere else in Spain, black eyes were so universal that any other colour in a lady's seemed as strange as if nature had given her three, instead of the usual number. I recollect one evening at a *tertulla* in Coria there chanced to be a very fair English woman present.

She was pretty and graceful enough to be remarkable even amidst much Spanish grace and beauty, but nothing was said of her fair skin and classic features. The buzz through the room about the lovely foreigner was—"*Mira, mira! aquella senhora tiene ojos azules!*" with a soft lisp on the last mellow word. "Look, look! that lady has blue eyes!"

During this winter measures were being quietly taken to promote the 'comfort, improve and preserve the health, and increase the efficiency of the British and Portuguese regiments. We were all in high spirits—cheered by the good news from Russia; and the reverses of Napoleon there, had a momentous bearing upon the war in the Peninsula, inasmuch as in all probability large draughts from thence would be required to reinforce the dispirited and diminished forces of their brethren in the north. The time was thus becoming favourable for a grand combined movement to push the enemy out of the kingdom. With secrecy and his usual consummate sagacity, did the great General who commanded us, prepare for the grand and final hunt over the Pyrenees.

There is a little old walled town called Galisteo, situated nearly equidistant between Coria and Placentia, where two of the regiments of our Brigade were quartered during the early spring months. At this place I was attacked by my old enemy the Tertian ague, which I dosed in the regular way with all the usual remedies for a fortnight—but all in vain—at twelve o'clock every second day my teeth began to chatter. Thinks I to myself—this open attack on the enemy will never do—let us try a manoeuvre. Accordingly, at half-past eleven I prepared a tumbler of hot spiced wine—ordered my horse to the door—got into the saddle and drank it off, and then proceeded in a canter over the extensive plains in the neighbourhood.

When it approached twelve, although the sun was powerful, I could feel the ague-fiend's cold fingers grasping my loins—I then put spurs to *Liberdade*—pushed him into a full gallop—and at length, by dint of perseverance and good management, I fairly distanced my villainous pursuer. I tried this plan with equal success the next time, and on the return of the third Tertian period, was delighted to find that at twelve o'clock my feelings continued comfortable—my spine did not turn into an icicle, nor my grinders commence their former hornpipes.

On my recovery, *comme d'ordinaire*, I reconnoitred the river at the bottom of the hill and picked up a considerable number of the usual dace and barbel. But the Spanish and Portuguese streams afford little variety and but poor sport, for, except the Bidassoa, I never met with a trout in any of them.

In April we moved to Placentia, a clean and respectable city with a singular cathedral, the front of which presents the architectural anomaly of the florid Gothic, Composite and Corinthian Orders. I rode, soon after our arrival, to visit the Convent of St. Justus, the retreat of the Emperor Charles the Fifth. The prior, who did the honours of the place, assured us that the story of the emperor having devoted much of his time to the regulation of watches was all a fiction. I could not much admire that great monarch's taste in the selection of a last abode, as I noticed many better-looking and as ancient convents in different parts of Spain. But the face of the country must have changed much since then.

During Passion Week we had a sort of religious tragedy performed every day by the clergy in Placentia, and on Good Friday there was a grand procession of images of the twelve Apostles as large as life, and the Virgin Mary dressed in garments of modern fashion, with a representation of the dead body of our Saviour, borne on a litter. These effigies were surrounded by a strong corps of priests and friars, chaunting most dolefully. This imposing procession issued from the cathedral, and visited, of course, every church and convent in the city.

The large windows of the cathedral and all the interior had been hung with black throughout the week, and the light carefully excluded. On Easter Sunday morning the principal inhabitants and a large number of British officers having filled the spacious interior to crowding and overflowing, the dark veil was suddenly withdrawn, amidst the loud and triumphant notes of a magnificent *Te Deum*—the sun shone in brilliantly through the painted windows, and all was at once, as if by magic, changed from the most melancholy gloom to the most gorgeous splendour.

On the following Monday we had a military spectacle at Placentia of a very painful nature, and in strong contrast with the rejoicings of the day before. A soldier of a British regiment was hanged before all the division for shooting his officer. This was followed by an extraordinary occurrence the same night. A man of another corps having dreamed that he saw the devil carrying away the soul of the murderer, and warning him to beware of a similar fate, was so impressed with terror that he awoke his comrade and told him his dream; and the poor frightened creature, appearing altogether to have lost his senses, started out of bed in his shirt, ran out of the house and drowned himself in the Xerte.

CHAPTER 15

Advance To Vittoria

For who is he whose chin is but enriched
With one appearing hair that will not follow
These cull'd and choice drawn Cavaliers to France?
                                        Shakespeare.'

On the clear, sun-shiny morning of the 19th of May 1813, the Corps of Sir Rowland Hill was put in motion from Coria and Placentia through the Pass of Banos towards Salamanca. The weather was beautiful; and this long march, which only ended in the Pyrenees, was commenced under the most favourable auspices.

The *Banos*, or Baths, from which this strong defile is named, are strongly sulphurous, and much and advantageously used in cutaneous diseases. Nature, in fixing their temperature, had been happy in her chemistry, as that good old experimentalist generally is. The heat is always about 105 degrees Fahrenheit, which, to most people's feelings, is precisely the temperature of a comfortable warm bath.

When we entered New Castille and approached Salamanca, the face of the country became very rich and tastefully ornamented here and there with much beautiful planting—graceful and undulating slopes were seen in all directions, which were dotted with clumps of tall and umbrageous forest trees; the whole country having very much the appearance of a fine park. All this was very pleasing, coming from dry, hot and treeless Estremadura. Still, as over all Spain, the population was concentrated in towns; and notwithstanding the beauty and fertility of the intermediate glades and valleys and rising grounds, they were without inhabitants, or only the demesne of the shepherds with their enormous flocks, or the hogs in quest of their food. What illimitable tracts of the finest land still lie fallow and useless in that lazy country.

On our approach to Salamanca, during the last day's march we perceived at a great distance, on the other side of the Tormes, a column of the enemy deliberately retiring. Lord Wellington was in front and immediately detached some cavalry and Horse Artillery across the river to cut them off. The day was clear, and when the advance of our division halted on a rising ground near the left bank, we had a distant view of the chase. A column of French infantry moved along resolutely, with some cavalry on their flanks and in the rear; and even when the guns opened and our dragoons came up, they could make no impression on the square of determined men who preserved their formation; but they dispersed the enemy's cavalry, and took about two hundred stragglers prisoners, with six guns, that we had the pleasure of seeing in the great square in Salamanca the same evening. This was a good beginning.

We encamped on the right bank of the Tormes, a mile from Salamanca; and in the evening a party of our officers rode into the town. Salamanca presents the appearance of a very venerable old place, solacing itself amongst magnificent ruins, by the consideration of its former greatness. The grand *Plaça*, or Square, considered the finest in Spain, is certainly superb; and the cathedral is a noble Gothic building, retaining still, two or three *murillos* that had been hid, and thus escaped French rapacity. This city has suffered terribly during the present war; for it has been almost all the time since 1809, in the possession of the enemy. We were shewn long masses of ruins, the remains of streets destroyed by Regnier, in the vicinity of the fortified convents, which had been attacked and captured last year.

We were unwilling to leave this fine old city so soon, but were ordered off the next morning, and marched six leagues to camp near the village of La Urbada; where we halted five or six days to give time to Sir Thomas Graham and the left of the army to advance. It was very plain that there would be no child's play this campaign, for large masses of men were moving concentrically on the main French communications with their own country, and prepared to overwhelm any isolated resistance. Concentration, then, must be the game of the enemy, and when the rival masses came within each other's attraction—to drop my figure and take another—then we should have the tug of war.

The whole of Sir Rowland Hill's Corps and the Light Division were here encamped. It was a fine game country—open, generally, but with picturesque copses and young woods here and there, affording ample cover and food.

The evening of the day we marched from Salamanca threatened to be a hungry one, for, except a little wine and two or three biscuits, our rations were out, and we could expect none till the next morning. My faithful Antonio, who hated hunger as much as Sancho Panza, looked longer-visaged than usual by an inch or two; and as the punctual Jonathan Wild heaped before the animals their ample allowance of glossy and succulent green forage, there was great temptation for wishing to be a horse for half an hour. Just as Antonio paraded the last biscuit and a cup of wine for my dinner, we heard a loud and prolonged shout close to the tent; and when I ran out to see what was the matter, I had scarcely cleared the tent-cords, when a hare that had been started in the purlieus of the camp—after a spring of some seven or eight yards, came bounding against my breast. It certainly was an ungenerous and indefensible act, and must be considered most cruel and barbarous treatment of a helpless prisoner so early in the campaign, but truth is truth, and must be told—poor puss was in the soup-kettle in five minutes.

There were certainly some doubts started as to property, but there were fortunately no game laws in Spain, and when the soup was boiling, possession was plainly in my favour. It would have been useless to enquire after the proprietorship, where, being a "*fera naturae*," none could have had existence. Through my whole life I have found the advantage of decision and promptitude of action, from matters of life or death, to the most trivial—even the splitting of a hair.

When the army was well advanced on the left, and everything ready, we broke up the camp and moved on Toro, where we crossed the Douro. The bridge had been destroyed, but was temporarily repaired, so as to admit of infantry passing over; whilst the artillery and cavalry crossed at a ford a little below. The water was inconveniently deep for the smaller baggage animals, and several poor donkeys got out of their depth and were lost. One of our soldier's wives, mounted on a good stout ass, swam her animal gallantly a quarter of a mile down the river, directing its course to a shelving bank on the proper side, which she reached in safety amidst a volley of cheers from the division.

On the 2nd of June there was a smart affair of cavalry near Morales, when our Hussar Brigade, consisting of the 10th and 15th Hussars, cut up a body of French dragoons—taking one hundred and fifty prisoners.

Meanwhile in every town we passed through the inhabitants received us joyfully, standing at the doors of the houses with pitchers of cool and delicious water in their hands, which they distributed to the thirsty men, and accompanying this kind attention with looks and expressions of cordial friendship, "*Viva los Inglezez!*" rung in our ears all the way. In this agreeable style we chased the enemy before us for the next ten days until we came close to Burgos, where they seemed inclined to make a stand, and some fighting of no great consequence took place on the heights near the town.

Next morning, the 13th of June, we heard a loud report, which was caused by the blowing up of the castle: a very delightful sound, for Burgos had become a word of ill omen, and we anticipated much trouble here. Little did we then know the dreadful loss the French themselves suffered by that calamitous explosion—the crushing of a column and the death of three hundred men. The precipitate destruction and abandonment of a place they had formerly successfully defended shewed fear and weakness; and we now could start, inspired afresh, on the glorious hunt across the Ebro.

When we approached Pancorvo, a place of some strength, on this celebrated river, situated on the high road from Burgos to Vittoria, we struck off by a path to the left; and after passing through a most difficult and formidable defile of two leagues, crossed the Ebro at the Puente d'Arenas without any opposition. Here was another proof that the French were much frightened, and quite bothered out of their judgment; for two or three hundred men might here have stopped our whole army, and gained a couple of days to enable the retiring masses of the enemy to retreat in better order.

We were now entering on a new country altogether, having a more northern character and differing totally in appearance, productions and the physical attributes and language of the inhabitants, from the parts of Spain we had so long occupied.

Fresh butter is a very rare article in the south of Spain, the want of which we had often deplored. At the top of this strong pass we met a great number of Biscayan *Paysanas*, dressed in tasteful and picturesque costumes; every one with a clean white osier basket on her arm, full of nice-looking prints of butter, neatly folded in vine leaves. As this was a luxury for which we all sighed, I bought immediately half a dozen prints; each with a good-looking Biscayan cow and calf on it in tempting *alto relievo*. The baggage being in the rear, it became a question of some importance, how I should stow away my prize. After some consideration, I took one of the pistols out of the holster, (for, though a man of a peaceful profession, it was just as well to possess these weapons:) put it in my pocket, and carefully stowed away the precious butter in its place.

We proceeded down the Arenas defile, admiring the grotesque shapes and threatening appearance of the huge masses of rock impending over our heads, until the valley of the far-famed Ebro began to open. The river here runs along a deep glen, with high perpendicular banks, covered with trees and rocks of the most fantastic configuration and extraordinary wildness. It is altogether a study for some *Salvator Rosa* amongst modern landscape painters, and I have often wondered, how it is that none of the Annuals have yet got hold of it.

When we crossed the bridge our division was obliged to halt for a couple of hours, until the road was cleared; having become jammed in the defile with part of the left of the army. The day was very hot and without a breath of air; but we thought of nothing but the new faces of our friends from the left, the display of accumulating force, and the splendid natural scenery with which we were surrounded. We arrived at our camp near Villacayo, about sunset; and on dismounting I was rather surprised at observing an unusual sleek and rather oily appearance on my horse's chest and forelegs, with patches of dust here and there, looking like dirty crust—in fact, his fore-quarters appeared as if they had been half-roasted after due flouring and basting. Immediately the nature of the sad calamity flashed across my mind, and I hastened to lift the holster-cover and find out the extent of the mischief. Alas! when I pressed upon the vine leaves they returned but a hollow sound! My firm and delicious butter had "larded the lean earth" of Navarre for many a league, and there was nothing but the green envelope remaining.

We advanced slowly from the Ebro on Vittoria, where rumour said the French army was collecting and appeared determined to fight. Our columns were now converging—the lateral routes were difficult for artillery—the enemy concentrating—it was therefore necessary to move cautiously. Some little affairs had taken place, and a couple of French divisions getting entangled in the intricate country to our left, had come in collision with our Light Division; but had effected their escape with trifling loss. The face of the country had altogether changed; and the bracing and beneficial influence of the cooler climate in the hilly region we were now traversing, was visible in the more robust stature, and fairer, and ruddier complexions of the natives.

All classes cheered us as we passed; and though, from the long march the men's shoes were worn out, and blistered feet among the soldiers, and sore backs among the horses and mules had become more numerous than was agreeable—the whole army was in the highest spirits. Certainly, ours had been a magnificent burst, without a check, from the borders of Portugal, across broad Spain, up to the confines of the Pyrenees. Scientific combinations had been carried into effect in distant, but harmonious movements of different corps and divisions of the Allied Army, without any disturbing impediment—all had been inspired with the confidence, and almost the certainty of success under their great leader: whilst two or three little brilliant cavalry affairs— the panic of the enemy—the acclamations of the inhabitants—and the beauty of the weather, were the scenic accompaniments of this first act of the grand drama.

CHAPTER 16

Battle of Vittoria

Now set the teeth and stretch the nostril wide,
Hold hard the breath, and bend up every spirit
To his full height——

                    Shakespeare.

Such was the deep impression produced by the important events of the 21st of June 1813, that everything of which I was that day a witness, remains as fresh in my memory as if it only occurred yesterday.

On that celebrated Sunday morning there was a little light rain about daybreak, followed by some mist and fog; which, however, did not last long, and were followed by a remarkably fine clear day. Having, from the commencement of the campaign, been attached as assistant to staff-surgeon Wasdell, in medical charge of the Second Division, I moved with the Headquarters, and thus always occupied a house when they were stationed in any village. On this occasion, as we all anticipated something to do this day, I awoke before daylight and looked out of the window at the camp of the division, half a mile below—but nothing was to be seen but the dense vapour—after another hour the mist was clearing away—the men were striking the tents and getting under arms—in half an hour more the whole was in motion towards the village of Puebla, where there was a bridge over the Zadorra, a branch of the Ebro, about two leagues from Vittoria.

It was early buzzed along the line of march that there would be hot work before night—the staff-officers as they moved with orders looked grave and somewhat excited, and there was a cessation of the usual chatting and joking in the ranks; which, though contrary to orders, was tolerated in those days, and with good reason, for it disguised and softened the tedium and fatigue of a march and kept the men in good humour.

As we were crossing the clear stream of the Zadorra at Puebla, (it was of a far different colour before the day was over,) I glanced into the water and saw a number of lively dace playing about, apparently altogether careless of the great events taking place in their neighbourhood. Morillo's Spaniards had seized the bridge and crossed before the British, and we now heard a little firing beginning on the heights on our right; said to be the scene of a victory gained by our Black Prince, and hence called "*los montagnos Inglezez*." By and bye the firing thickened—we passed one or two dead bodies of French soldiers on the road, and the whole column moved towards the table land above the river in compact order.

When we reached the top a grand and spirit-stirring spectacle met our view. We saw the extensive line of the whole French army posted on a range of heights about two miles off, in order of battle, with Vittoria in the centre. The position appeared to be nearly four miles in length—the greater part of the troops were in column—some in line; and the artillery was disposed in batteries on the most commanding points. Numbers of mounted officers were moving about slowly from one part of the field to another.

This was the first time I had seen a powerful army prepared for battle; and the sensation was exciting, exhilarating and intoxicating! I was young and ardent, and felt strong emotions in anticipating the approaching combat and the probable discomfiture of those imposing masses. I longed to join in the struggle and "throw physic to the dogs."

When our division had advanced along the high road to Vittoria, within long cannon-range of the enemy's position, we were ordered into a field to the right, and then halted. The word was then given, "With ball-cartridge prime and load!" In the meantime Sir Rowland Hill and a large staff, including the staff-surgeon and myself, rode forward to a small height whence there was a better view; but the crowd of mounted officers having attracted a shot from one of the enemy's nearest batteries, the greater part of us were ordered away, and only Sir Rowland and two or three of the senior officers remained.

Soon after this the brigade of Colonel O'Callaghan, consisting of the 28th, 34th and 39th regiments, attacked the village of Subijana d'Aliva, and having there suffered a heavy loss, I was ordered to the assistance of their surgeons.

We collected the wounded in a little hollow, out of the direct line of fire, but within half musket-shot—unpacked our panniers and proceeded to our work. This Brigade had, I believe, between four and five hundred men put *hors de combat* in the course of an hour; so, we were fully employed. A stray cannon-shot from a distant battery would drop among us occasionally, by way of a hint to inculcate expeditious surgery. After one of these unpleasant visitors had made its appearance, a young chirurgeon of my acquaintance, who is still living, became so nervous that although half through his amputation of a poor fellow's thigh, he dropped the knife, and I was obliged to finish. At my suggestion he lay down on the grass, took a little brandy, and soon recovered and did good service the whole day. Spring wagons were in attendance, in which we placed our patients and sent them to Puebla, the nearest town, where Dr. McGrigor, then at the head of the medical department of the army, had made the most judicious arrangements for their reception and comfort.

When we had attended to all the wounded of this brigade that we could find; including a large proportion of officers—several of the latter hit mortally—a message came to the staff-surgeon from the heights on our left; for a long time the scene of a bloody struggle: that there were a large number of wounded, and that they required more medical aid. There the 50th, 71st and 92nd regiments had been sent early in the day to assist Morillo and his Spaniards; but, strong reinforcements having joined the enemy on the hill, those gallant corps were hardly pressed and suffered great loss. I was again detached and ordered up the hill on this urgent requisition.

I had been so entirely occupied, professionally, for three hours, that I was quite in the dark as to the state of the engagement; except that, latterly, the sound of the firing appeared louder and closer than at the beginning. As I rode up to the higher ground, therefore, I endeavoured to see how matters stood, but I could make out no more than that some heavy firing both of artillery and musketry was beginning on the French right: the relative situations of their force and ours, as far as I could observe, was the same as before. I was pleased to hear the firing on their right, as I knew it was occasioned by our left wing coming into play.

As I galloped up the hill, a round shot passed so near my head as to make me bob instinctively; though, as Napoleon is made to tell his guide at Waterloo, the bob might as probably be in the line of the ball as *out* of it. At any rate there is a precedent in point, in the case of the great Marshal Turenne, for bowing to "a gentleman of that family:"

yet, that illustrious commander seems to have gained little by his civility, for a cannon ball killed him at last. I certainly made the best bow the time would permit; and as the shot plunged into the ground about ten yards from me, I felt no particular sorrow at its death and burial.

The death of Colonel Cadogan of the 71st, was as glorious as that of Wolfe. After he received his mortal wound, he reclined with his back against a tree, his glazing eyes directed towards the enemy, and his last moments, like Wolfe's, cheered by the account of their defeat. After witnessing this fine scene with deep emotion, and working hard for two hours with the medical officers of the Brigade, I returned according to my orders to the depot of the wounded near Subijana, from whence I had set out. Everything now appeared changed—the firing was far advanced towards Vittoria—the enemy had abandoned several points of his position and seemed to be in full retreat.

In front of the village of Subijana d'Aliva, which had been taken early in the action, by Colonel O'Callaghan, there was a wood, about four hundred yards off, which was full of French *tirailleurs*. Between this wood and the village was a large cornfield, without any hedges or enclosures, or cover of any kind more than the green wheat: and here I could not help thinking then, (and I am of the same opinion still ;) that there had been very needless exposure and wanton waste of life, without the possibility of any good being derived from it. I saw myself, early in the action, parties detached from the village, where they had good cover, into the open field, and there fruitlessly and fatally contending with the fire of the *voltigeurs* from the wood and the artillery from the main French position.

So ignorant, even, did these brave men appear of the true danger of their situation, that they enhanced it a hundred fold, by absolutely *grouping themselves* in little masses through the field for mutual protection; each of which objects formed a target not to be missed by covered infantry, and scarcely by artillery. Such was the loss sustained in this point, that in one part of the field, not more than about two acres square, I counted one hundred and fifty men either killed or very badly wounded.

Here the staff-surgeon, two other surgeons and myself, set to work afresh, after swallowing some wine and biscuit; and here we remained collecting, dressing, amputating and sending to the rear, till seven o'clock.

When our work was done and we had picked up every wounded man in the neighbourhood of Subijana, we mounted our horses, that had been regaling themselves all the time in the wheat, and pushed on for our own division, now, with the whole army far in front. At this time the French were flying all across the country, having been cut off from the main road to France by Tolosa. We passed Vittoria a mile on our left, where the plunder of King Joseph's Treasure and Baggage was going on, and our dragoons were getting drunk with his *Tokay*. By swerving a little *from the right* here, literally as well as figuratively, I might have picked up something valuable; for a brother *medico* who did, met with a drunken dragoon who had just rifled a carriage of two bags of money, and not being able to balance both and himself together on horseback, tossed him one, containing a thousand French Crowns.

It was now sunset and the pursuit still continued. Most of the enemy's artillery and baggage had fallen into our possession, but there was still one large convoy, escorted by some cavalry, that appeared to have a fair prospect of escaping in the approaching darkness. A troop of Horse Artillery, commanded, I think, by Captain Bull, galloped up and unlimbered within range on a rising ground near the road, whilst we stopped to see the result. The convoy was at this time entering a small defile in the road, when the captain pointed the first gun, exclaiming—"Now for the first carriage." He made a beautiful shot, for the ball killed the two front mules in the leading carriage, and thus stopped the whole; and before the impediment could be removed our dragoons were up, and the whole convoy was captured.

After such a day's work there was a great deal of confusion at nightfall—soldiers and officers straggling about, unable to find their corps. The staff-surgeon, a Mr. Frith, chaplain to the Forces, and myself, strayed about the country three hours after dark, fruitlessly endeavouring to find the Second Division. Regiments, brigades and even divisions, became intermingled; and it was at least mid-day after the battle before this confusion was remedied. In the course of our wandering that eventful evening we also got our humble share of the plunder; for we picked up a sheep, a keg of cognac brandy, and I stumbled over a piece of superfine cloth that made me afterwards a pair of inexpressibles, of which I was sorely in need.

We might have laid in a good library of French novels on this occasion, for the road was strewn with them thickly for miles; together with public and private letters, military rolls and returns, prints and packs of cards. And not merely the road but the fields on each side, to a considerable extent, were covered, and how this most extraordinary scattering and dispersion took place is a problem I never could make out.

After wandering till midnight to no purpose, we fell in with some stragglers of the Buffs and 57th, who kindled a fire, skinned and dressed our sheep, and broiled us a chop upon the coals. They divided their biscuit with us, and we gave them a share of our cognac. After this we wrapped ourselves in our cloaks and slept profoundly after a good day's work.

The reunion of a corps of officers after a hard-fought and successful day, is an event of a highly interesting and affecting nature—all the worser passions and tendencies are subdued, under the influence of the exhilaration of the moment, the joy of escape from the late danger, and the delightful consciousness of recent good conduct and intrepidity. Other of the social charities, also, mix with these emotions—sorrow for the dead and sympathy with the wounded. Then follows from each his own peculiar adventures—disquisitions of the general conduct of the business on both sides—the bearing of particular corps—individual feats of heroism—killed and wounded, &c., until the whole battle is fairly fought over again. After mutual congratulations and enquiries, I was pleased to learn that although the regiment had its fair share of the fighting, and had lost about fifty killed and wounded out of three hundred and fifty, only two officers had been hit, and neither mortally.

I forgot to mention in its place that when ordered up the hill to assist the medical officers of the First Brigade, I met with my old friend Dudgeon, the tall officer of the 71st. He had a presentiment of being killed; and, having a good deal of money in his possession, he begged I would take charge of his purse, and have it forwarded to a relation in case of anything fatal. I endeavoured to laugh him out of his gloomy forebodings, but it was in vain, and the purse was confided to me; which being a good large one, and full of gold, was no small annoyance during that busy day. I had great pleasure in restoring it to its worthy owner a short time afterwards.

On the evening of the 22nd of June, we started again on a fresh chase; but as the enemy were then in light marching order—having been relieved from the encumbrance of baggage and artillery—there was not much chance of catching them.

At Salvatierra we found that three bedridden old people had been murdered that morning in cold blood by the retreating enemy, apparently without any provocation, and from shear wanton cruelty. We pushed them without any respite as fast as the horrible state of the roads would permit—broken up as they were by rain and the previous passage of the French disorderly masses—up to the strong defiles leading to the Passes of the Pyrenees, some of which they attempted to defend.

Nothing could be more ardent than the demonstrations of joy in every town we passed. This was the first time since the era of the Black Prince, that English soldiers had been seen in these romantic and secluded valleys, and we were absolutely treated as if we had dropped from the sky on some benevolent mission. As we marched through the streets the windows were crowded with women, cheering and waving white handkerchiefs, and tossing out loaves amongst the soldiers: whilst the men stood at the doors, serving out wine to the officers, or handing goblets of deliciously cool water from their porous earthen vessels, to the men. For with nice discrimination, they would not give wine to the soldiers without the permission of the officers. All this time the bells of Churches and Convents would ring away with all their might.—Shouts of "*Viva los Inglezez!*" filled the air, whilst every little urchin that could utter a sound, mingled his shrill treble in the general acclamation.

On the morning of the 6th July, the Corps of Sir Rowland Hill entered the fine vale of Bastan—quite a gem amongst the Pyrenean valleys—which was still occupied by two French divisions, whom we proceeded to drive from several successive positions. There was a good deal of desultory fighting all the day—for the enemy had still some stores in the pretty town of Elizondo, which they were withdrawing, and consequently defended the approaches to the place with great obstinacy. The staff surgeon and myself, moved with the advance; having our mule and surgical panniers close up, so that we very frequently attended to the wounded amongst the light troops engaged, before they could be seen by their own medical officers, who were with their regiments, a little way in the rear.

In one case, where it was necessary to amputate the arm below the elbow, the patient, a fine-looking Light Bob of the 50th Regiment, said not a word whilst I was operating, but bore the pain with the greatest fortitude. At length when it was all over, he looked at the mutilated hand, and exclaimed with an oath—"I would bear it all ten times over, if I could ram that bloody hand into my piece, and blow out the cowardly villain's brains with it that shot me!" On inquiry we learned that the poor fellow had good reason for his indignation; for it appeared that the Light Company of the 50th had surrounded a farmhouse in which about a score of French had sheltered themselves. Finding they could not escape, they held out a white handkerchief from a window, as a signal of surrender—the firing then ceased on both sides; but when the first of the English, who happened to be my patient—entered the door, a rascal discharged his musket at him—shattering his hand which he threw up instinctively to save his head. The remainder then made a rush out, and in the surprise of the moment most of them escaped.

We entered Elizondo late in the evening, with the Light Companies and Staff of Sir Rowland Hill, whilst skirmishing was still going on at the other end of the town. Head Quarters were fixed here during the night; and the same tumultuous acclamations of joy and welcome met us as everywhere else. Indeed these demonstrations were peculiarly piquant, and somewhat hazardous to the people of this fine town; for the joy-bells began to ring whilst the enemy were yet in sight, and their glad sound and that of the firing struck on the ear together in singular and exciting unison. There was utter fearlessness of danger, and the most disinterested kindness to us, therefore, in the hearty welcome these good people gave us.

In riding through Elizondo, and passing a good-looking house, a Priest saluted us, and begged we would do him the favour of spending the night at his house; and sharing the dinner he had prepared for some of his "*carissimos amigos, los valientes Inglezez*"—his most dear friends, the valiant English. As we were both hungry and fatigued, it is scarcely necessary to observe that we required little pressing. So our horses were put in a comfortable stable, and were soon up to their ears in provender, whilst we sat down to dinner with his reverence and his niece—a very pretty *muchacha* of seventeen. Our good host had just dug up his plate, and some famous old wine that were buried in the garden four years before; and, *certes*, we passed a merry evening with this jovial and patriotic ecclesiastic.

In the exhilaration of his joy for the emancipation of his native valley from the French yoke, under which it had so long groaned—assisted, perhaps, a *little* by the "*Vinho vejo*" the excellent priest got slightly fuddled, and sang us several Spanish songs. In return he asked for "God save the King" from us; of which he said he had heard much by report. My friend, Wasdell, having declined, and the priest being very urgent, the task devolved on me—and very much did the old gentleman admire and encore my poor performance—and very sweetly did the sloe-eyed *muchacha* lisp out her pretty admiration of it—until the evening,—like all parties, and the chorus, ended happy and glorious.

Next day we advanced to Maya, one of the grand Passes, amidst the same exciting circumstances of partial fighting and cheering by the villages through which we passed. As the evening advanced, and the French retired to the top of the Pass, there was literally an engagement in the clouds; both parties being enveloped, and a bickering musketry fire kept up amidst their picturesque and voluminous folds. There were not many casualties; but staff surgeon Wasdell and myself, thought it necessary to sit up all night in the church of Maya, to dress any wounded that might be brought in.

At sunrise the next morning. Lord Wellington passed through the village to the front; and in riding past the church, he sent for one of the surgeons. I went out, and for the first time, had the honour of a short conversation with his Lordship. He was pleased to hear that so few men had been hit, and that their wounds were, for the most part, slight. He then rode on, saying courteously—"Good morning—go on with your duties."

The enemy descended to his own side of the mountain during the night, and in the morning the British Troops stood proudly on their summits, looking down upon the fertile plains of Gascony.

CHAPTER 17

Fighting for a Week

Thus come the English with full power upon us,
And more than carefully it ns concerns
To answer royally in our defences.

Shakespeare.

When the French were fairly driven over the Pyrenees, and the British Army established in those strong gorges of the mountains forming the Western Passes, the Head Quarters of Sir Rowland Hill remained at Elizondo, whilst those of Sir Wm. Stewart, commanding the Second Division, were advanced to Maya, a small village about a mile from the Pass. Staff Surgeon Wasdell and myself were attached to the latter, and were quartered in Maya.

We passed the first fortnight very pleasantly; riding about and exploring the magnificent mountain boundary where we were stationed. Unfortunately, clear weather was not common in those elevated regions, and it was not very often that we could enjoy that bird's-eye view of France which we anticipated in approaching the Pyrenees.

At this time Napoleon, finding that matters were going on very badly in Spain, and that his brother had been ignominiously driven from the kingdom, sent Soult from Germany, to set them to rights. He invested him with the high Commission of Lieutenant of the Emperor, and directed him to organize the army afresh, and chase the Leopard, as he called the British Lion, from the presumptuous position he had taken on the borders of the "Sacred Territory," or holy land of France.

Soult travelled with great expedition—stimulated by a desire to distinguish himself, and wipe off a score of affronts he had received from the English. He soon re-established order and confidence in the beaten troops; proceeded to throw strong masses of troops in the immediate vicinity of the Passes of Roncesvalles and Maya; and then lost no time in making a determined effort to pierce at once our extensive line in two or three places with superior force, then take the different posts *en revers*, beat them in detail, relieve Pampeluna and St. Sebastian; and, following up his advantages, force the English back to the Ebro.

According to the best military opinions, this was all well conceived and practicable; but one or two elements of success in the calculations were only contingencies, not very likely to happen. The French must fight far better than they had yet done, and the British worse—Lord Wellington, too, must be bothered in his nerves and fail in judgment.

Sunday again was desecrated by the belligerents—in fact, that period of religious repose seemed almost purposely chosen for strife and slaughter. On Sunday morning, the 25th July, we were alarmed at Maya, by a report that the enemy had appeared in force near Los Alduides; a post in the mountains, three leagues to our right, whilst everything appeared quiet in our immediate front. On receiving this intelligence. Sir Rowland Hill, Sir William Stewart, and the whole of their staff rode off to the right; and the day being fine, almost everybody in Maya followed in the same direction; so that at twelve o'clock I found myself the only commissioned officer in the village.

Being an unusually clear day, I mounted my horse and rode towards the top of the Pass, where a brigade was encamped, to take a peep at Gascony. On my way I met the *Bat-men* of the 50th, 71st and 92nd regiments on their mules, going to the rear for forage—an unhappy journey for their masters. The day was still as well as clear, and as I proceeded I heard a shot or two from the top of the mountain, which in a few minutes thickened into a sharp fire of musketry. The picquets, I found, had been attacked and driven in; and when I reached the top I let the troops in motion to support them. It soon became plain that the enemy was in great force—pushing strong columns up the hill, preceded by a swarm of light troops.

It was the Count D'Erlon who commanded here, and the business had been managed skilfully by the feint at Los Alduides—this being the real point of attack. Notwithstanding a gallant resistance, the count established himself with fourteen or fifteen thousand men on the summit of the mountain, to the right of the Pass; and in two hours from the time I had left Maya, the camp of the First Brigade, (whose mules had gone to forage,) tents and contents—the town of Maya—the Headquarter baggage—the commissariat and hospital stores, &c.

&c., lay below him absolutely at his mercy.

It was very plain that without energetic measures I should lose my own goods and chattels with the rest: so—

Self-love and social being here the same,

I galloped down the mountain to Maya, at some risk of my neck. None of the staff had yet returned, and the servants were in great confusion and alarm. I immediately directed everything to be packed up and sent to the rear with the greatest expedition; and took upon myself the whole responsibility. Some of Sir William Stewart's servants were a little refractory, but were soon cowed into obedience. I also hurried away the commissariat bullocks and biscuit, but had no mercy on the rum, as the mules employed in removing it would be wanted to carry the wounded, that were now beginning to drop in. Accordingly, the commissariat conductor set to work staving the casks, and we had soon a stream of old Jamaica running down the steep street into the rivulet at the bottom, fit to turn a mill. I wonder how the little fishes liked their grog.

The wounded now began to arrive fast. Many had been dressed by their own medical officers, but a large proportion required in-stant attention, which was paid them as far as the time and my ability permitted—the slighter cases being sent away on foot, and the more serious ones on mules. The enemy allowed us longer time than I ex-pected in these operations; so that when a few of his sharpshooters be-gan to make their appearance close to one end of the long straggling street—the Governor—my humble self—with the last of his convoy, was moving leisurely, and without any confusion, out at the other.

Dire was the consternation of the poor inhabitants when they saw us retreating through the beautiful valley of Bastan, which had been the scene of such gratulation and triumph on our advance three weeks before. Many of them, male and female; and almost all the inmates of the convents—abandoned their homes and retired with the army. It was a painful sight to see the poor nuns quitting their convents and mixing with the troops in the dusty roads—their pale faces hectic with unwonted exertion, alarm and exposure. To the credit of our men, it ought to be told that great kindness, tenderness and inviolable respect were shewn to them on this retreat—the soldiers carried their little bundles and helped them along; and it was pleasing to observe the unsuspecting confidence with which many of these old ladies trusted themselves and their portable property to the protection of our rough grenadiers. Assuredly, it was a high compliment to the character and disciplined the British Army.

As we passed through Elizondo, a large proportion of the population joined us in the retreat. I called at the house of our worthy host, the priest, who had so kindly entertained us, but had only time for five minutes' conversation at the door. Poor fellow, he looked very desponding, and I have seldom seen a greater contrast than between his lugubrious face now, and his jolly and rubicund *phiz*, when roaring out the chorus of "God save the King." The pretty niece had been sent to a relation near Pampeluna. When I bade the fine old fellow goodbye, I advised him to bury his plate and wine once more, adding that we should all be back in a fortnight again to tax his hospitality— "*Oxala a Dios! Oxala a Dios!*" "God grant it—God grant it!" and then embracing me warmly and giving me his benediction, we parted.

We halted, confronting the enemy, the whole of the next day, that we might cover a movement of troops in the rear from the neighbourhood of St. Sebastian to Pampeluna, or its immediate front; and in the evening the whole of Sir Rowland Hill's Corps retired through the mountain pass of Lantz in the same direction; but such had been the difficulty of this lateral movement that we fell in with the Seventh Division on the narrow road, and some confusion was thus occasioned. As night fell it began to rain heavily, and became so pitch-dark that no object could be seen a yard off; and the horses were trusted to pioneer their riders along the side of the mountain, where a false step would be destruction. My pole-star was the white tail of the staff-surgeon's horse, just before me, of which I caught an indistinct observation now and then, when I stooped and looked attentively. At length both divisions were obliged to halt in the middle of the night on the ground where they stood on the mountain side—from absolute inability to proceed.

From the 25th July to the 2nd August, was a week of hard fag and fighting. Sir R. Hill's Corps continued to retire before the Count D'Erlon on the 27th, 28th and 29th—still shewing him a formidable front—covering the movement of troops to the right, and keeping up a communication with Lord Wellington's main force in front of Pampeluna. During this time the staff-surgeon and myself, being both well mounted, were not idle. On the night of the 29th, Sir Rowland posted his corps on a strong range of heights, five or six miles to the left of the position of Lord Wellington, and there anxiously awaited orders and the course of events.

At daybreak on the morning of the 30th, everybody was on the *qui vive*. We had been apprised of the repulse of the enemy on the 28th— the 29th had passed quietly; but we all expected something decisive on the 30th. As soon as it was clear, the staff-surgeon and I mounted and joined a large assemblage of staff, who, with Sir Rowland at their head, were on their way to a high hill, two or three miles to the rear; whence they hoped to be able to descry the important operations on the right. For, by this time, a very heavy musketry fire and cannonade was going on there merrily; and we could see a cloud of smoke, but nothing else. After remaining on the hill nearly an hour, and plying his glass perseveringly. Sir Rowland ordered a movement of the whole corps to the rear—apparently with the object of connecting himself more closely with the Headquarter Force, from which he was too distant.

However, this order was countermanded; for, soon after the reconnoissance from the hill, and Sir R. and his staff had returned to the strong ridge where the troops were posted, the heads of several of the enemy's columns were seen moving simultaneously on the position— coming from our right, and apparently determined to attack us. Light troops were immediately thrown down the steep and wooded side of the hill, and other active measures taken to give them a warm reception; but it appeared to me at the time that Sir R. anticipated being forced, and did not like to hazard the loss of his artillery; since, though a brigade of English and another of Portuguese artillery were close in the rear of the heights now threatened, they were not ordered up; although they might have done considerable execution amongst the approaching columns, of which we had from the top the finest view possible. But, for this, no doubt, there were the best reasons at the time.

The French dashed at the hill gallantly—throwing out clouds of skirmishers, who forced ours back on the main body at the top. At one point near the centre of the position, they pushed so hard that the Light Companies came running in, close to where the general and his staff stood; and it required their utmost efforts to turn them back. On this occasion I distinctly saw Sir Rowland himself, turn right about face, three or four of the 50th Light Company, who, panting with heat, and with faces blackened with powder, had been forced up by superior numbers. Additional skirmishers were sent down at this point, and the enemy was repelled.

It was now three o'clock, and the sound of firing, far to the right, was still heard occasionally; though the interest in affairs there, had been for some hours absorbed in what was going on before our eyes. Hitherto the enemy's efforts had been unsuccessful; but he was now seen prolonging his attack to our left, where from the great extent of the position few troops could be posted. At length, after a long struggle, the French established themselves on the hill, and prepared to advance along its crest; when Sir R. Hill retired his corps in good order to another position two miles in the rear.

This was a sharp affair, although, from the thick cover, there were few casualties, and the regimental medical officers attended to their own wounded. The staff surgeon and myself were close up to the line at the top of the position, all the time the action continued, with our mule and surgical panniers; but we had little to do, except look at the fighting.

In the evening news arrived of a severe engagement having taken place that morning, a little way in front of Pampeluna, where the enemy had been defeated with great loss. At the same time an order arrived for S. S. Wasdell, to detach a medical officer to the village of Barrioplano, to collect there the wounded of both armies, and forward them in spring wagons to Vittoria. I was sent on this duty, on which I was employed five days and nights, with scarcely an hour's intermission—divorced from my baggage and Antonio; whose face I had not seen for a week already—and employing a heap of wheat in a barn, when I was permitted to snatch half an hour's sleep—literally as bed and board—for I got nothing else to eat.

A very large number of wounded were brought in here on this occasion; all the disposable spring wagons with the army, and a great many carts and mules, being employed in collecting them at the villages near the extensive field of action, and conveying them to the Church of Barrioplano; (situated on the high road, a mile from Pampeluna,) as to a central point. Here their wounds were examined—dressed—the limbs that required it, amputated—and the patients again put in the wagons and sent to Vittoria. Such was the urgency of circumstances, that for the first two days, I had no medical assistance here; but afterwards abundant aid was afforded by two cavalry assistant surgeons.

During this busy time, my brother assistant, Shekelton, (a worthy man, now flourishing in Dublin, [as at time of first publication]), rode over to Barrioplano, to consult me respecting the case of our mutual friend and brother officer, Major Goldie, who lay at a village three or four miles distant, under his charge, desperately wounded by a musket ball through the lungs. It appeared that the ball had lodged somewhere in the chest, and the symptoms continued alarmingly dangerous. The patient had been most judiciously and tenderly treated, and his life saved, hitherto, by enormous bleeding, to the extent of three hundred ounces in two days.[1]

It chanced one morning that two spring wagons full of wounded French officers, prisoners, were brought in, and very soon after, two more with our own people, principally of the Chasseurs Britanniques; a corps composed chiefly of foreigners. I was then busy in the church with a batch of wounded soldiers that had arrived earlier, and as the principle was—first come, first served; without respect of persons, I directed that they should be put in a neighbouring house, until their turn came. When I proceeded with my surgical apparatus to take care of the new arrivals, I found them in a state of the most violent excitement; abusing each other with the grossest epithets, and very nearly come to fisty cuffs. The French officers were vilifying their countrymen of the Chasseurs—calling them "*sacrés traitres! lâches esclaves d'Angleterre!*" and their opponents were retaliating with equal heat, gesticulation and bitterness.

It was altogether a most laughable scene—most genuinely French; and I believe that nothing but the paralysing effects of their wounds restrained them from an actual engagement. When I entered there was a momentary pause; but the quarrel broke out afresh in two minutes. I used all my eloquence to pacify them, but fruitlessly—still the mutual objurgations were bandied about with astonishing volubility and vehemence. At last, perceiving that the case was becoming desperate, I seized my instruments, directed the orderly to carry away the tray of plasters and bandages—bade the pugnacious gentlemen good morning, and requested them to fight it out. This calmed them at once; they were then dressed and despatched in separate wagons to Vittoria.

When this tedious and harassing duty was over, and no more wounded were brought in, I proceeded once more to Maya, and found the Divisional Headquarters again established in that village, and the troops occupying their old posts on the hills. Great was the comfort of meeting my baggage after a long destitution of clean linen, and an

---

1. I have great pleasure in adding, that this very gallant and valuable officer recovered after this prodigious loss of blood; though he still carries the ball in his lungs. He now commands the 11th Regiment in Lower Canada, and notwithstanding some very severe winter marching to and from New-Brunswick lately, I had the satisfaction of seeing him this very day in good health.

intolerable beard of twelve days' growth.

In the course of the month of August, we moved with Head-quarters, to the classic Pass of Roncesvalles, after a romantic march amongst the clouds enveloping the tops of the mountains. We were treated with a thunderstorm on the way, with the novelty of the lightning playing harmlessly *below* us, and the odd bellowing of the thunder from beneath. By the way, is not **χμραῖῶττος** , from the frequency of these storms, the true etymology of Pyrenean? Pyrène, the lady who has the credit of having given her name to the mountains, lived a long way off, in Andalusia; and there is no evidence, that I am aware of, that she was ever connected in any way with the Pyrenees.

At this time the siege of St. Sebastian was going on: at length on a very tempestuous day, the place was stormed, amidst the rival thunder of the sky and the batteries. The storm extended all over the western limb of the Pyrenees, and blew down half the tents of our division.

We continued at Roncesvalles, until the surrender of Pampeluna, left Lord Wellington at liberty to push into France. We then, once more, moved along the mountains to the Pass of Maya; where, on the morning of the 10th November, the corps of Sir Rowland stood, like greyhounds in the slip, ready for a dash at the position of the enemy in front of Bayonne.

CHAPTER 18

Invasion of France from the Pyrenees

Fresh legions pour adown the Pyrenees—
It deepens still————————

Byron

A full hour before daylight, on the morning of the 10th of November, did we wait for the firing of a gun on the extreme left, which was a signal for our advance; whilst high feelings were working in many bosoms. After the lapse of three centuries the banner of St. George was once more to be unfurled in Gascony, where, except Calais, it had waved the latest on French soil; and other victories might now rival the glories of the olden time.

As soon as the long-expected echoes rolled amongst the mountains, the column was put in motion and crossed the frontier, whilst a heavy firing was going on to our left. We marched about two leagues, until within cannon shot of the fortified heights above the small stream of the Nivelle, which had the honour of giving its name to the battle. Here we halted in front of a very strong part of the fortified hill, which our division was to storm; and as soon as a brigade of the Sixth Division, immediately on our left, had done their work by attacking a redoubt on the top and taking it. General Byng's Brigade pushed up the steep and abbatied hill at one place, whilst the Light Companies of the division and the two other brigades assailed it at other points.

When the leading regiment of Byng's Brigade reached the plateau on the top, they looked such a handful that a French column opposed to them deployed into line and prepared to charge: but, though I saw their officers cheering them on gallantly, they would not move, but kept up an irregular fire, which, being badly aimed, did far less mischief than it ought to have done. When more force came up and the brigade formed and advanced, the enemy's line wavered, not metaphorically, but visibly and materially; and after two or three oscillations they broke and ran.

There still remained a small field redoubt with two guns in possession of the enemy. These were fought by an officer of artillery, a sergeant and a few men, and being loaded with double charges of grape knocked over our people fast. Lieut. Colonel Leith, 31st—my friend Lieut. Colonel Nicol, 66th, and Ensign Dunn of the same corps, at the head of three or four men, charged this work and carried it in good style. Indeed, the three officers took it themselves; for they cleared the ditch with a running leap, and dropped down amongst the garrison, before a man could enter to assist them. As they jumped in, the artillery officer and his men jumped out; but not with impunity. Leith, a Hercules in strength and figure, knocked the red-headed officer down with a brick-bat, but his cap saved his skull, and he managed to scramble up and get away. Not so lucky was the sergeant—he dislocated his shoulder in the leap—was taken prisoner, and I set his arm to rights immediately afterwards.

We lost a good many people in storming this hill. The Light Companies, commanded by Major Ackland of the 57th, suffered severely—every officer was hit, and the major killed. The death of his pretty little spaniel, that had during the action amused itself by barking at the dust the balls raised as they struck the ground—preceded its master's fall only by a few minutes. I had to lament the loss of two friends in the regiment who were mortally wounded.

Our time was occupied professionally, till late in the evening. When we had done, and were in quest of some refreshment, a well-dressed woman accosted us, apparently in a state of the greatest distraction and distress. She told us she lived in the village of Espelette, immediately under us at the bottom of the hill—that Morillo's Spanish Division had got into the place, and were beginning to burn and plunder, and her husband had run away and left his family, from dread of the Spaniards; and that she had come out alone, trusting in English generosity, to beg for protection. She implored us, therefore, to accompany her home, as our presence would save her and her family from the Spaniards. This poor woman was so importunate, that, after obtaining permission, we went to her house. The town was in the greatest alarm and confusion, and part of it on fire; but on this being known a regiment was sent down to extinguish the fire and turn out the Spaniards. A party of plunderers visited our residence, but instantly decamped when they found it in possession of British Officers.

Our family were also labouring under distress of a peculiarly severe nature from another cause; and in meeting accidentally with two English surgeons, Madame Dupré was piously pleased to consider the circumstance as specially ordained by Providence. By a most unlucky fatality, poor Jacqueline, one of her daughters, during the action on the hill happened to be looking out of the window, listening to the firing, when a grape-shot from a gun in the redoubt last taken, which was turned on the enemy as they ran down to the town—smashed her elbow-joint. Amputation was inevitable and I took off her arm the same evening, and am happy to add that the stump was perfectly well in a fortnight.

It would be a graceful finale to add that Mademoiselle Jacqueline was very pretty. Truth forbids this; but she was amiable and grateful; and after she had recovered the first dreadful shock of such a loss, she presented me with a handsome purse of her own netting as a fee.

Madame Dupré had a good house and was in comfortable circumstances: she treated my friend and myself with great kindness, and made us very comfortable. She had a full cellar, and there was one cask of very rich and clarety *vin du pays*, which she forced me to accept for distribution amongst my brother-officers in camp. Accordingly, next morning I had a *levée* of their servants, with tins and tea-kettles and all kinds of vessels to carry it off.

On the 13th of November, Sir R. Hill made a reconnoissance of the enemy's force at Cambo, a small town on the left; bank of the Nive, which had been partially fortified. When we got within shot. Colonel Nicol and myself happened to be riding together at the head of the brigade, mixed with the band of the Buffs, when a ball plunged amongst us, knocking over three or four musicians. In five seconds they all jumped up again, amidst great laughing, for they were all unhurt; and the only sufferer was the big-drum, which was mortally wounded; and its fall upset the two men that carried it—whilst they overthrew the two others.

We stood in line two or three hours exposed to fire. As General Byng was passing on horseback where I chanced to be looking on, *en amateur*, a shell alighted within seven or eight yards of us both. With much coolness he remarked, "There is no danger—throw yourself off;" shewing me the example. When we had embraced mother earth about two seconds, it burst; and I caught a glimpse of a large fragment describing its parabola over our heads, but at a safe distance.

This was escape the second: I had also a third that day. There was a small house, a little in rear of the centre of our line, where we were attending the few wounded; for we had only four or five, notwithstanding a long cannonade—a brother *medico* and myself were amusing ourselves with a glass, looking out of a window in the upper story, at the French Artillerymen on the rampart of Cambo. When it came to my friend's turn to take a peep, he exclaimed—"By Jove they are pointing that gun direct at this house—we had better go downstairs." We descended accordingly, and had scarcely reached the bottom when we heard a crash over our head; and instantly a shower of tiles came down from the roof. The bombardiers had at last found the range, and had pitched a shell into the very room we had quitted, which killed a poor woman in the house who had brought water to her wounded husband. Thirty or forty officers' horses were picquetted round the house—the noise and the falling of the tiles sent them galloping, with broken bridles, in all directions.

At this time I was witness to a very strange occurrence. The commanding officer of the Buffs, a regiment in General Byng's Brigade, left his corps, then under fire, and came half a mile to the house above mentioned, to inquire after one of his men that had been hit. Unfortunately he met the brigadier, who gave him a cool look—his personal courage being more than suspected—but said nothing. When the lieut. colonel had made the necessary inquiries, and staid as long at the house as he could with any decency, he returned to his regiment. But, in half an hour back he came to the house, and his unlucky stars again threw Byng in his way. This time he was peremptorily ordered to his post, with the withering appellation he deserved, and strictly forbidden to quit it at his peril.

The individual here alluded to, after one or two subsequent demonstrations of cowardice, saw his name in the *London Gazette* one day; but not in the way of promotion. The Prince Regent, in the name and behalf of George the Third, gave him his gracious permission to go about his business. He and two other *chefs de bataillon* were turned out of the army.

Lord Wellington having resolved to invest Bayonne more closely than he had yet done, and to cut off its communications with St. Jean Pied de Port and the Western Pyrenees, Sir R. Hill crossed the Nive at Cambo, on the 9th December; and on the 10th, we found ourselves in a good country, a mile or two from Bayonne.

Byng's Brigade was quartered in and about the village of Vieux Mougerre. The house allotted to me, was that of a substantial farmer, half a mile from the village. As the inhabitants were always glad to have officers quartered on them; thus saving them from the plunder they were taught to expect from the soldiers—the farmer's wife told me she was enchanted to see me in her house. In fact the old lady was overpoweringly civil and complimentary both to myself and my countrymen; assuring me she always loved and respected the English, who were "*une nation superbe*"—so brave, and so good, and so religious. "*Tenez*" she went on—"*regardez cette église*"—pointing to the cathedral of Bayonne—that magnificent edifice was built by your Black Prince—"*assurément que oui; par votre grand Prince Noir.*" She then told me that everything in the house was at my disposal, and concluded by inquiring what she would prepare for dinner—recommending particularly—as the best article in the larder—"*une oie magnifique, si grasse et si tendre.*" So the magnificent goose was forthwith ordered to be put on the spit.

Having some professional duty to do, I left my horse in charge of the farmer—the servants and baggage being still in the rear—and went into the village. When my work was over, I met, on my way home, a hungry-looking young ensign of the regiment, on whom I took compassion, and invited him to share my dinner. It was now near sunset, and close on the hour the worthy dame told me the meal would be ready. As we approached the house we heard sounds indicative of something wrong about the establishment—cocks and hens were screaming and cackling—dogs were barking—pigs were grunting—with similar ominous noises, that made us hasten our steps to find out what was the matter.

As we entered, the first object we beheld was—O sight of horror! a drunken German soldier of the 60th regiment, bearing away the spit and innocent goose, streaming with its rich juices, in his unhallowed clutch! The frightened farmer had shut himself up in the barn, but the gallant dame had contended bravely, although fruitlessly, against the Philistines. When we entered, she brightened up wonderfully, and just found breath enough to say, "*Il y a un autre voleur dans la cave—la cave—la cave!*" The goose-thief bolted out of the back door, spit and all, the instant he descried us, but I soon caught him, whilst my companion dived into the cellar and found the other in the very act of suction at a wine-cock.

The disturbed bird was then remanded to its roasting evolutions before the fire, whilst we conducted our prisoners to the provost martial, and had the satisfaction of seeing them receive fifty lashes each. Farther and more severe measures had been in contemplation, but we requested that this might be the maximum of punishment; considering the cruel disappointment of the rogues, and that they had got their goose the wrong way.

It is scarcely necessary to add that, after all this, we enjoyed our dinner and some good *vin du pays*. The goose richly deserved the encomiums of its mistress; and I doubt whether a finer or sweeter bird had been cooked since the deliverance of the Capitol.

CHAPTER 19

Battle of Orthes

The cannons have their bowels full of wrath.
King John.

We were not destined to remain long quiet in our good quarters round Vieux Mougerre. Soult feeling uncomfortable at the closing in of the allied troops, attempted to dash through the investing line with superior force at a favourable point; and thus play over again his game of the Pyrenean irruption of the last summer. He first attacked the left of the army, on the high road to St. Jean de Luz; but could make no impression during two days hard fighting. He then withdrew all his troops into Bayonne, and on the morning of the 13th December, made a vigorous effort to overwhelm Sir Rowland Hill.

The business was well planned; and had the troops fought out the combinations of their general, we might once more have been obliged to retire behind the Pyrenees. They advanced from the city in great apparent confidence, and assailed the picquets about daybreak; but when they found, early as it was, that the whole British and Portuguese force of 14,000 men, were sternly awaiting them, the first burst of excitement evaporated. Although, as to numbers they were very much superior, with a strong fortress at their back, they were well beaten, up to the very glacis, and two of the field pieces they ventured to bring out were taken—one of them by the Light Company of the 66th Regiment.

Our fine little commander, Sir Rowland, much distinguished himself on this occasion, and was praised for his conduct and arrangements by Lord Wellington, when he arrived from the left in the afternoon, with the 6th Division, as a reinforcement.

I had good professional practice on the 13th, for we had twelve or thirteen hundred wounded. Some wounds were frightful, yet the patients recovered: and I may mention amongst the worst, the case of Captain Bulstrode of the 66th regiment, who received a grape-shot in the lower jaw—the ball carrying away one side of the jaw entirely, and burying six teeth in the tongue, which I extracted at the time. This officer recovered, and I had the pleasure of dining with him afterwards in London.

Immediately after the action, hospitals were established at Cambo and Espelette, and I was sent to the latter town to take charge. I had about twenty officers and nearly two hundred men under my care for the first three or four days, when a senior officer relieved me in the responsibility, but I continued doing duty at the place. The weather was fine, though cold: I was young and active, and felt delighted in not having an unemployed moment the whole day. As the slight cases recovered and went to the front my patients often sent me a fat turkey, or a goose, or a sucking pig, or some such matter, as a fee, which varied the toughness and monotony of the eternal rations. Amongst the wounded under my charge here was Lieut. Colonel Leith of the 31st, who had been shot through the arm by a musket ball. The ball grazed the brachial artery; but the coats of the artery—like the man they belonged to, were made of good stuff, and not easily torn. The colonel recovered in a few days; and, as he got the English papers, his quarter was the News-Room of Espelette.

It chanced that a turkey of great merit was sent me one day from Mougerre, which I requested Colonel Leith and two other convalescent officers to partake of. When I went out to my work, after an early breakfast, I gave Antonio very particular directions as to the cooking of the dinner, which he promised faithfully to follow; and I proceeded to my daily laborious task; comforted occasionally, when I had time to think of anything but my patients, by the pleasant perspective at the close of the day. The hour of dinner was six; and when I returned a quarter before, I found—

Quis talia fando temperet a lacrymis?

the immaculate Antonio lying prone and dead drunk in the kitchen—the beautiful bird unspitted and unstuffed; and the elements of soup, in the shape of ration-beef, lying beside it on the table!

But patience is a panacea for human miseries; and this was one far overtopping the long catalogue in Beresford's book. I repaired to Colonel Leith and told him the calamity that had just happened, and requested the loan of his cook to repair it. The beef was put in the pot and the turkey to the fire incontinently—a fresh batch of English papers had arrived, with which the hungry *quartetto* amused themselves. *En fin*, about eight o'clock dinner was announced; and notwithstanding the unpromising appearances two hours before, everything passed off well and happily.

About the end of January 1814, I rejoined my regiment at Mougerre, in good order for some recreation, after a six weeks' fag—which we had in private theatricals, reconnoitring Bayonne, and thinning the Gascon wood-cocks.

The view of the Pyrenees from Mougerre was very fine—a hundred and twenty miles of their western extremity were distinctly visible; forming a magnificent snowy rampart of considerable elevation, but a nearly equal surface. To me they then appeared of great elevation, but since that time the Himalaya Chain has dwarfed them into mole-hills.

The very wet weather we had had lately quite spoiled the roads, so that the advance of the army into the interior was much retarded; at last Sir Rowland's Corps was put in motion on the 13th of February—the division of General Harispe retiring before us. On the 15th, the enemy made a stand on the strong hill of Garris, near St. Palais. We arrived in front of this position, after a long march, near sunset, and everybody expected that the attack would be deferred till the next morning: but Lord Wellington at that time came up; and being apprehensive that Artillery would be mounted on this formidable height next day—ordered it to be assailed immediately.

Four columns then dashed into the ravine and up the steep side of the hill; which was one blaze of fire from the enemy's skirmishers behind the trees on its face, and the main body along the top. This was, for the greater part, as harmless as common fireworks—the balls going over our fellows' heads; but as it became dusk the effect was strikingly beautiful. Our troops soon reached the summit—scattering the French division and taking a few hundred prisoners. Fifty or sixty unfortunate wretches concealed themselves in a house at the top until the affair was all over, and our men had piled their arms and were kindling their night fires; when they sallied out in a body, and attempted to escape down the hill.

At the first rush our soldiers seized their arms, which were loaded—pursued them with a loud cheer, and shot or knocked down almost every man. They were stripped soon after—for this process takes place in a very short time—and I recollect when the moon rose seeing their plump white corpses scattered over the field. In the morning we were all shocked to see their bodies mutilated of their fair proportions, and all the fleshy and protuberant parts cut clean off down to the bone. How this happened none could say; although a report was current at the time that a certain ingenious regiment of Byng's Brigade had metamorphosed the poor defunct's hams into pork, and exchanged them with the Portuguese troops for rum. One of our officers averred that he heard two of the culprits chuckling at the trick.

I happened to be the first surgeon at the top of the hill that evening, and, of course, was in great demand. General Byng carried me immediately to see his *aide-de-camp*, Captain Clitheroe, who was dreadfully wounded. I found this fine young man with his hand smashed, and a ball through his breast, which had cut a large artery that I could just reach with my finger, and, I believe, I prolonged his life a couple of hours by continued pressure. This young man was much beloved, and his death greatly deplored. His end was serene and calm, and he died in my arms with the resignation and fortitude of a soldier and a Christian. He was buried next morning on the hill where he fell with due military honours.

This was altogether as shewy a little piece of fighting as I ever witnessed. The brilliant musketry along the side, and from the crest of the hill—the cheering of our men as they mounted—the continued advance of numerous bugles—the roar of our artillery reverberating in long echoes from one side to another of the deep ravine at the bottom—all was very fine and grand.

We proceeded the day after the action through St. Palais, and after some sharp skirmishing and fording two or three Pyrenean tributaries of the Adour, encamped on the other side of the Gave d'Oleron, opposite to Orthes, on the 25th of February. Next morning another officer and myself, in the course of an exploring ramble in quest of eggs or poultry, found an old man badly beaten and bleeding in a farmhouse that had been robbed the night before, by a marauding party of our soldiers. The temporal artery had been cut by a blow of the robber's bayonet. It was tied up—the matter reported immediately—search made for the criminal; and the soldier, having received a cut in the thigh from the wounded man, was soon discovered. Summary justice was the practice in those days; and, after identification of the prisoner, he was hanged in presence of the assembled division the very next evening, on the bough of a tree; and after being suspended forty-five minutes, I was ordered to ascertain whether life was extinct, that the men might not be kept longer in the cold than was necessary.

On the 27th February, we were early under arms. At eleven o'clock an *aide-de-camp* arrived with directions for Sir R. Hill to ford the Gave above the town of Orthes, and advance round the left of the French position. All this time a heavy cannonade and hard fighting were going on about two miles to our left, on the other side of the river.

Immediately all was in motion. We soon reached the ford, which was covered by some of the enemy's light troops in a thicket on the opposite bank. A couple of guns galloped down, opened on them with grape and soon dislodged them—the grape whistling through the covert like duck-shot. The division then rushed into the ford— five or six shells dropped amongst us in crossing; but, I believe everyone was extinguished in the water without doing any mischief; and in the course of an hour the whole were formed on the right bank and ready to advance.

We moved on very imposingly round their flank; and at length discovered that they had abandoned their position, and were making off with great speed; which the appearance of our column tended materially to quicken. At the village of Montbrun we joined the cavalry and the advance of the other English divisions in pursuit: at this time the whole French Army, despairing of effecting their retreat, if they preserved their formation, had broken irrecoverably, and the face of the country to a great extent was covered with a dense mass of fugitives. All arms were mingled—artillerymen without their guns—cavalry without their horses, and infantry without their arms—were flying pell-mell—helter-skelter—whilst our Light Artillery were pouring shrapnel shells amongst them, and thus increasing the general terror and confusion. In short, no flock of sheep ever fled more valiantly; whilst in the bright and beautiful evening, the sun's broad face, throwing the yellow beams horizontally on the fugitives, and lengthening their flitting shadows to fantastic proportions, appeared to be playing luminous antics over the scene, as if in derision.

We followed the rout till dark: a little before dusk they got into some small degree of order, and made a stand at a village on a strong hill, with a small river in front; and opened with two or three guns. But they retired in the night.

Lieut. Colonel Dodgin, my former refractory patient at Badajoz, now commanded the regiment. Whilst riding at its head over "a sea of arms"—for upwards of ten thousand stand were flung away—a fine ornamented pioneer axe, with a long handle and glittering head, struck his eye and his fancy. Thinking it might be useful at the night bivouac, he threw it over his shoulder and rode on. At this moment one of Lord Wellington's *aides-de-camp* passed; and on seeing an officer of large stature, and imposing appearance—mounted on a great war-horse, with an immense axe on his shoulder—he stopped and asked his name. When I told him, he inquired farther—"Is that, then, his usual weapon in action?"

"O yes;" was the reply, "and the colonel, like *Coeur de Lion*, often cleaves his man to the chine."

The *aide-de-camp* rode away, primed with a good story for the commander of the Forces.

When we halted about dusk, in column on the road, a shot from one of the enemy's guns on the hill where they rallied, struck the ground, rose again and knocked over one of the soldiers' wives, who always managed to keep up with the regiment. I ran to her immediately, but found there was only a graze, and slight contusion on the shoulder. At first she was sadly frightened; but when I assured her there was no harm done, she was so delighted that she pulled a fowl out of one enormous pocket, and half a yard of black pudding out of the other, of which she begged my acceptance. I cannot say I pocketed the fee; but we regaled on it at our bivouac that evening.

After three days' pursuit, the French again made a stand on a strong hill, near the town of Aire, on the Adour, and after rather a sharp but short affair, they were driven from their post. They had no guns on the hill, but fired from three or four, placed on the high road, quite over their own position, so as to drop the balls amongst us as we advanced by a narrow causeway, flanked by the Adour, to attack it. I did not observe or hear of any casualty from the round shot; though thirty or forty plunged into a muddy field on one side of the road, and the river on the other, sufficiently near to splash some of our faces. My gallant friend. Col. Dodgin, led the Light Companies of the division in his usual dashing style, but not with his usual luck. He was hit by a musket ball in the side, and tumbled off his horse.

The ball was fired by a fellow behind a hedge, not twenty yards off. It struck him above the right hip, and was cut out directly opposite, over the left. Yet there was no danger; for it hit a button of his coat, and was thus deflected from its direct course through the abdomen into a curve outside the muscles, but through a deep course of fat. The impression of the two figures on the button remained stamped accurately on the ball; which had made a nest for itself, lined with thirteen bits of cloth.

On the advance from Aire the lieutenant colonel requested that I might be permitted to remain to take care of him; which was courteously granted by General Byng. Immediately I got a good quarter for my patient, and established myself under the same roof.

CHAPTER 20

Peace

They now to fight are gone;
Armour on armour shone,
Drum now to drum did groan—
To hear was wonder,
The very earth did shake,
Trumpet to trumpet spake—thunder to thunder.

Drayton.

My duty at Aire did not alone consist in attending my patient. We had several other wounded officers who were placed under my charge. A number of French prisoners wounded at Orthes, whose surgeons had deserted them, and a ward in the British Military Hospital were also entrusted to me; so that my hands were pretty full. Dr. McGrigor, Head of the Medical Establishment of the Army in the Peninsula, was then at Aire; and he generally gave his officers plenty of work when humanity and the public service required it; and made them do their work well too.

I may observe here, in passing, that I never had a more painful charge than that of the hospital of French wounded. Whether the state of their wounds was attributable to faulty surgery originally, or to rough conveyance from the field of action, or neglect since their arrival here—or, what is probable, to all combined—the fact was, that nothing could be more deplorable than their condition;—the smaller wounds were foul and sloughing—the men's health very bad—and most of the stumps were what we technically call sugar loaves; with the bone projecting and little union; all of which required re-amputation.

One morning when I was quitting the British Hospital, a cart was driven to the door from the Second Division, then quartered five or six leagues in front, containing a French and an English dragoon—the latter being the worser case was attended first. This man, Corporal James Buchanan of the 13th Light Dragoons, carried with him a written certificate from his commanding officer, stating that he had been attacked the day before by three French dragoons—whom he fought individually—slaying one outright; putting the second to flight badly wounded, and wounding and capturing the third, who came with him in the cart. Buchanan had received fifteen wounds; in the head, face, arms and body: his nose was cut off and one bone of the forearm cut through.

It is needless to add that I paid the tenderest attention to this glorious fellow; patched up a jury-nose for him as well as I could—and, I am happy to say, left him convalescent, and in the best intelligence with his prisoner, who slept in the bed by his side.

On the 2nd of April, my patient being quite recovered, we marched to join the army. Our route lay through a fertile and pretty tract of country on the left bank of the Adour; but the road was the ugly, straight and elevated *chaussée*.

At the clean and handsome city of Tarbes we were detained three days, from apprehensions of some straggling French cavalry in our neighbourhood. Our march on the whole was very agreeable—the dazzling Pyrenees on our right—good roads—an interesting country—civil people, and now and then the excitement of a white cockade.

On our way to the neat little walled town of Mirande, a soldier belonging to a detachment we were taking to the front, had been guilty of theft with some violence to an inhabitant; and, after due enquiry, was ordered by the colonel to be punished at the end of the day's march. As soon as the people of Mirande heard this, a deputation of about a dozen of the principal ladies waited on the colonel in a body, and begged forgiveness for the culprit. They pleaded so eloquently and earnestly, and looked so pretty on this mission of charity, that nobody could refuse their prayer.

The mayor gave us a billet on the best house in the town, the owner of which, a fine old gentlemanly man, was an ardent Bourbonist. The lady of the mansion was one of the most enthusiastic legitimists I ever met: but there was a tinge of ferocity about her politics that did not comport well with the gentleness of her sex. She shewed me a list of Buonaparte's Marshals which she kept, with black marks opposite the names of those that had died or fallen in battle; and she added that, during the last ten or twelve years, pricking these funereal notices on her chart had been one of her highest enjoyments. She was a firm believer in the illegitimacy of the King of Rome, and told us stories of Marie Louise and Josephine and Napoleon that would some years before have made me blush; but now my visage was already sunburnt into a suffusion far more rosy-brown than agreeable.

We had an excellent dinner and many bumpers of *Champaigne* afterwards, to the health of Louis the Eighteenth—the Prince Regent—our hostess and the ladies of Mirande: with a pretty *bal* in the evening.

Again on a Sunday, and Easter Sunday too, the 10th of April, when we reached Auch we heard a very heavy firing in the direction of Thoulouse, which lasted all the forenoon. Nobody appeared to heed it; and this general unconcern of the inhabitants at a serious engagement in their neighbourhood, was in strong and disagreeable contrast with the intense feeling of interest I had witnessed under similar circumstances at Campo Mayor, two years before.

We heard next day at Gimont of the Battle of Thoulouse; and the people blamed Soult much—believing that he had no business to expose a great city to the horrors that might result from a defeat in its very suburbs. Everybody appeared confident as to the speedy downfall of Napoleon, and Bourbon demonstrations became stronger as we advanced. At length at L'Isle en Jourdain, just as we entered, the mayor returned from Thoulouse with the astounding news of the deposition of Buonaparte and the restoration of the old family. In five minutes the inhabitants collected in the square, and when the mayor read from the *Moniteur* the official intelligence, quite a grove of white cockades burst on the sight simultaneously, amidst deafening shouts of "*Vivent Louis dix-huit! Vivent les Bourbons! Vivent les Anglais! Vive Lord Vellingtonne!*"—and then we all repaired to the church to hear a grand *Te Deum*. In the evening a ball on a great scale was given by the mayoress, to which, of course we were invited, and treated with the most marked friendliness and attention.

We entered Thoulouse amidst universal demonstrations of the most lively joy, and when we reached the great square we witnessed a most extraordinary sight. A fine colossal statue of Napoleon, of white marble, stood on the top of the pediment of the Capitolium—the grandest building in the city, which occupied one side of the square. A strong rope had, that morning, been rove round its neck, and there were two or three hundred people hauling away below with shouts and execrations.

What a spectacle! A crowd of wretches that would have sunk into the very earth at the frown of the living man, but two short weeks before, were now perpetrating this brutal indignity on the beautiful sculpture of Canova!

The magnificent statue resisted with characteristic tenacity for a long time, but at length gave way amidst an infernal yell of execration—tumbled from its lofty site upon the pavement, and was broken into a thousand pieces.

We found workmen busily employed all over the city in substituting "*Royale*" for "*Imperiale*" and obliterating every where the poor persecuted great Ns. The Bees also—Napoleon's emblem—were flying off rapidly, and every external mark of the fallen dynasty fast disappearing.

In the evening we went to the theatre—the play was Henry the Fourth. The demonstrations of Bourbon loyalty and the Anglomania were quite overwhelming. Lord Wellington was present. As soon as he made his appearance in the Royal Box the whole audience stood up—the performance stopped; and actors and spectators joined in three of the loudest peals of acclamation I ever heard. Cries of "*Vive Louis dix-huit! Vivent les Anglais! Vive Lord Vellingtonne! Vive le Roi George!*" were a thousand times repeated. It was all like magic.!

This was a week of extraordinary excitement, and unusual festivity at Thoulouse. Balls and *fêtes* followed each other rapidly. Lord Wellington resided in the Palace of the *Préfet*, and was attended by a French guard of honour. Still, amidst all this gaiety there was a cloud yet in the military horizon, and a possibility even of some more fighting. Soult, sulky and obstinate, continued with his army at Carcassonne, and refused to send in his adhesion to the Bourbons. It was very generally believed at Thoulouse, that, previous to the battle of the 10th—he had received intelligence of the abdication of Napoleon; but conceiving his great antagonist was at length at fault, and confiding in the strength of his position, and desirous to end with *éclat*, he had concealed the news, and thus caused a great and wanton effusion of blood.

On the 16th of April my patient and I rejoined the regiment at Ville Franche; after a march from Thoulouse, along the Canal of Languedoc, cut by Louis XIV, to connect the Garonne with the Mediterranean. In the vicinity of the city the country is woody, rich, and well cultivated; but as we travelled eastward it became flat, bare and ugly.

The clear morning of the 18th found the whole of Sir Rowland Hill's Corps assembled under arms, near Ville Franche, in a state of considerable impatience to learn the *ultimatum* of the Duke of Dalmatia, which had been peremptorily demanded by the Duke of Wellington. To fight, or not to fight, was the question. After remaining four long hours in this suspense—whilst the eyes of all were strained on the road to Carcassonne, we saw a coach coming along at a rapid rate, escorted by four English, and four French Dragoons. These were cheered as they passed, and we soon learned that the Count de Gazan and one of Lord Wellington's *aides-de-camp*, were in the carriage, charged with the adhesion of Marshal Soult to the Bourbon government. Thus, then, ended our fighting.

Soon after, our brigade moved to a small village named Pourville, about two miles from Thoulouse, where we remained six weeks, and a very agreeable time we passed; in good quarters, with a cheap and plentiful market at hand—a fine country—the most pleasant season of the year—and *fêted* nightly by the loyal Thoulousians, in the first fervour of their joy at the restoration of the Bourbons.

On the 27th April the Duc D'Angouleme entered Thoulouse amidst the unbounded acclamations of the whole city. The streets were lined with the Allied Troops—a cortege of British General Officers, and a very numerous band of mounted gentlemen of the city, escorted him through the streets to the cathedral, amidst a royal salute from our artillery; whilst thousands of bright eyes beamed smiles upon him from the windows, and a whole forest of white handkerchiefs were waving over his head.

The ladies of this ancient city pique themselves not a little on their superior birth, beauty, and accomplishments—with much justice, I believe. They aver that the coarseness of the Revolution never tainted society in their aristocratic town; but that there—as in a chosen asylum—the gentle manners and fascinating *politesse* of the old school sought refuge. Certainly very many delightful persons were to be found there at the time of our visit; and many were the British officers that succumbed to the graces of the fair Thoulousians—married outright, and surrendered at discretion.

The Bishop of Thoulouse had a country house near Pourville, in which two other officers of the regiment and I resided. There was a large garden, and a neglected fish pond that was full of frogs; and in the heat of the day these reptiles used to come to the surface of the water to look about them, and take the air: and when they found the sun too hot, they would wisely poke their heads under the broad leaf of some flag, or water lily, which served the purpose of a parasol. A great bull-frog enjoying himself in this position, looked somewhat like a fat Hindoo reposing under his *chattah*.

A venerable old servant of the Bishop, who wore a queue of the longitude of Louis the Fifteenth's time, was left to take care of the establishment. When he wanted a little game for his dinner on a *jour de fête*, he was accustomed to visit the pond with a branch of a willow for a fishing rod, and a piece of thread and a crooked pin for hook and line; a petal or two of a pink or carnation, serving for a fly. When he bobbed this over the heads of the frogs, some hungry fellow would rise at it like a trout, and be pitched out on the bank; but very often the old *maître d'hôtel* would have his work to do over again, after all. For the pin having no barb, Mr. Frog would very generally soon extricate himself and hop away—the more vivaciously for the prick in the jaw he had just received. Very often I have enjoyed a hearty laugh when sitting in a neighbouring summer-house, and witnessing the antics of *Messire Jean* and a fugitive frog. *S——é!* he would exclaim, when it got off, *S——é bête!* and then deliberately taking off his spectacles, and laying down his fishing rod, he would address himself to the race. If his game hopped towards the water, escape was easy; but if the reptile was bothered as to the *locale*, and took a course into the interior, its hind quarters would infallibly be roasting on a skewer, or stewing in a *fricassée* in a quarter of an hour.

CHAPTER 21

Embarkation for England

Good classic Lewis, is it, canst tliou say,
Desirable to be the Désiré?
Why wouldst thou leave calm Hartwell's green abode,
Apician table and Horatian ode,
To rule a people who will not be ruled,
And love much rather to be scourged than schooled?

Byron.

We left our pleasant quarters near Thoulouse, on the 3rd of June, to march to Bordeaux; there to embark for England. Our route lay down the left bank of the Garonne; one of the most rich and lovely tracts in France. The marches were short—the inhabitants overwhelmingly civil, and we had a ball every night.

The Portuguese Oporto Brigade, composed of three fine regiments, that had long associated with our second division, and fought many a well contested field together, accompanied us part of the way. When we arrived at the town of Bezace, where their route turned off to Bayonne, the officers of Byng's Brigade gave a parting entertainment to the Portuguese officers. This final *fête* was marked by a remarkable display of cordiality and brotherly affection between the companions in arms. British airs were called for by our friends, and we gave them Portuguese in turn; whilst suitable toasts were cheered in flowing bumpers, until it was time to go to the ballroom. These regiments had secured the esteem and respect of the British soldiers by their gallantry in the field, and general good conduct. Next morning we marched early; and when we came to the cross-roads where we were to separate, the old fellow-campaigners, officers and men, embraced and exchanged affectionate *adieus*: and as we moved in different directions, loud and prolonged cheers answered each other in peals and echoes, until they melted away in the distance.

And there too, excellent and faithful Antonio! there didst thou separate from thy master, and wend thy way to thy native Coimbra, and to astonish the untraveled simple ones of the Mondego by the relation of thy various adventures. Honestly didst thou always serve me; and though in a moment of weakness thou didst once err, and forget to put the turkey on the spit—this one fault was lost amidst thy general virtue—it was only a spot in the sun. I do believe, my poor knave, that thou didst not soon forget thy master: for of this the tear that fell upon my hand when kissing it at parting, was a pledge!

We reached Bordeaux on the 18th of June, and encamped with the Light Division soon after, on a large heath, four leagues from the city, waiting for ships of war to take us home.

Three more weeks of gaiety and enjoyment were passed here. We were in long arrears of pay, which were discharged at Bordeaux, at the rate of two months per week: consequently we had plenty of money to spend—and there were not wanting tempting objects in that fine city to beguile us of it. Indeed, our superfluous cash was especially relished by the Bordelais at that time; when, from the stagnation of trade, and general commercial distress in France, their beautiful quays were mantling over with grass, and the richest vintages remaining unsold in their cellars.

We had then a snug mess of eight, at a *château* in the neighbourhood of the camp, occupied by my commanding officer and former patient, Lieut. Colonel Dodgin. Here, I regret to have to tell, that from the unfortunate abundance of claret and cash, the life we led was less characterised by strict temperance than by several other virtues. Half of the mess used to go every three or four days to Bordeaux, stay a night, and return from "the smoke and noise of Rome" to the cool shades of our *château* garden—letting the remainder have their turn the next day.

Once when a party had been in town to see a Mademoiselle Georges—a tragedy beauty of thirteen stone—play Ophelia in the French *Hamlet*—and had returned as far as the commencement of our avenue, we saw two odd-looking figures in white, moving about the garden—spouting and gesticulating—which we were much puzzled to make out. On a nearer approach they turned out to be two of our officers; who, under the influence of wine the night before, had shaved each other's heads, and made a mutual vow to walk about the garden in white sheets until we arrived, under a pecuniary penalty from the defaulter. They had walked about thus half the night, and all the morning and forenoon; and lucky was it for these mad-caps that there was good shade, else the small remains of their brains would have evaporated altogether.

About this period we witnessed another triumphal entry of the Duc D'Angouleme at Bordeaux; which was even more brilliant than at Thoulouse: but there was an unfortunate accident which damped the joy. A British brig of war, moored near the quay, killed one of the crowd with the wadding of a gun, in firing a salute. I was standing on the balcony of the American Hotel, facing the river, when the misfortune happened close to the house. I then heard several cries from the alarmed multitude—"*C'est exprès—C'est exprès*"

I suppose that in the memory of man—at least since the useful invention of money—horses and mules and asses were never so cheap in Bordeaux as in the memorable month of June 1814. All the chargers of the officers commanding—many of them sorry chargers—the horses and hacks of the officers—the mules of everybody, and the donkeys of the soldiers' wives, were in the market at once. All were sellers—the remainder buyers—particularly towards the end of the month. By the exercise of a very small proportion of foresight I perceived that this was inevitable, and as soon as we arrived sent two horses and a mule to market.

I had a black savage horse, named "Barbary," sold to me by Lieutenant Strenowitz, a German Officer, since honourably mentioned in Napier's *History*. His crimes and misdemeanours had been manifold; but he was a shewy animal—of a glossy black, and a strong, active and perfect horse, in the fullest sense of the word. Yet, on more than one occasion had he so ungenerously behaved, that the order to slay him was on the point of being issued. Once, when I visited his stall and put my hand on his neck to caress him, he seized me by the breast with his teeth; and if I had not made a desperate struggle to escape, and pommelled him well with my fists about the eyes—but, especially, if my vest and shirt had not given way—he would, in all probability, have dragged me under his forefeet and killed me outright. I had the red marks of his broad teeth on my breast-bone for three weeks.

When my servant was shewing off Mr. Barbary in the Horse Market, an elderly French gentleman was struck with his appearance, and asked his age and price. He then moved round him, scanning his points critically; and afterwards made the man walk, trot and canter him. This ordeal being passed, the buyer examined the joints, feet and eyes; and after a pinch of snuff, proceeded to inspect his mouth. Barbary had hitherto undergone these liberties with tolerable *equanimity* and forbearance; but when this last freedom was taken with his person he uttered a fierce yell, seized the poor man by the shoulder and proceeded to worry him as a terrier would a rat. The crowd ran to the rescue—sticks and stones and curses dire rained on Barbary, and he was obliged to drop his prey before he had committed actual homicide. Of course, all chance of sale for that day was over—my servant jumped on his back immediately and brought him home.

I sold this man-eater at length to a Spanish *Capitraz* of Muleteers for two *doubloons*, though he was worth ten. He soon commenced his tricks with his new master, but he met with his equal in the biting department. These hardy fellows are accustomed to ferocity as well as stubbornness in their mules, and know well how to subdue them. The last time I saw Mr. Barbary, his new master was clinging to one of his ears *with his teeth*; whilst a muleteer was belabouring his ribs on the other side with a cudgel. Under this pleasant treatment he was leaving Bordeaux on the road to Spain; and, for aught I know to the contrary, the discipline might have been kept up half the way to the Pyrenees.

We sailed in the *Rodney*, 74—for Cove; and soon after in the *Chatham*, 74, to Spithead, landed at Gosport and marched to Bristol.

CHAPTER 22

Leave of Absence

My native Land—Goodnight.
                    Byron.

As soon as I could obtain leave of absence, I proceeded to my native vale in the North of Ireland, where the three months soon passed away amidst the kindnesses and warm hospitalities of a circle of relations and friends. "*Non cuivis contingit adire Corinthum*" Everybody had not travelled in those days; and a traveller, particularly a campaigning traveller, was then thought an acquisition to society. Before I went abroad I had a very humble opinion of my own merit; but I now rose rapidly in self-esteem. It may be well believed that I told all my Peninsular stories to the best advantage—described the battles I had been in to the Militia officers—re-amputated shoulders for the doctors—detailed the dresses of the Spanish ladies, and expatiated on their floating movements and pretty lisp, for the edification of my fair acquaintances; and descanted on the respective merits of the vineyards of the claret country for the wine-bibbers. In short, when my leave was nearly up, I found myself the centre of a considerable knot, and already expanding into some importance.

My visit was in September, and it may be well supposed that the verdant banks of the Esk, the scenes of my earliest and purest pleasures, were again often explored. My favourite stream was as clear, as cheerful, and as populous as ever, and the banks as velvety and green as before. There was little change around me; but what an alteration a few years had made in the microcosm within. I felt a saddened but sweet enjoyment in visiting points especially hallowed by association with the memory of my departed cousin; and all that I had since seen of womankind appeared vain, empty and worthless, compared with her simple elegance, expressive beauty and pure affection. Yes—the poet's exclamation is the very truth of nature. It *is* sweeter to remember those cherished ones death has snatched from us, than to mingle in the breathing world.

In the course of my rambles, angle in hand, it was agreeable to discover that I had not been forgotten by the good yeomanry of the vale of Esk. I was frequently coaxed out of a flying advice, when there happened to be any sickness in the house, by the flattering exordium— "Oh! shure he's the clever young docthor that used to be fishing here about, and playing with the childer—Och, Lord bless him, he's jist come from the wars, and shure its himself can tell us what we're to do to Judy's futt." After this it was impossible to refuse.

A renewal of leave was asked and refused. I therefore lost no time in joining the regiment at Newport in the Isle of Wight. Soon after, a detachment of eight officers and one hundred men was ordered to march to Chatham and embark to join the first battalion in Bengal. I was directed to accompany it.

We embarked on board the *Lord Melville*, Indiaman, in February, but were baffled by contrary winds and calms ail the month of March, and lay tumbling about in the Downs until the 3rd of April.

Few things can be more annoying than remaining weather-bound in port with every arrangement for the voyage completed. But, about the middle of March an event occurred, which dispelled for a while the monotony of our life at the stupid anchorage—Buonaparte again in France! When we heard he had landed, most persons on board thought the attempt was madness, and that he would be instantly apprehended and shot. When, however, news arrived that the Garrison of Grenoble had joined him, matters looked a little more serious; still the general opinion was that the daring invader would be stopped at Lyons, whither the Compte d'Artois and Marshal Macdonald had repaired to organize a loyal force: only one person was credulous— my humble self. Well, he reached Lyons, and the troops cheered and joined, instead of shooting him. But there was yet Ney, with his iron cage ready, and pledged to pack him up and send him to the Thuilleries.

In this state of suspense we left England, and many and various were the arguments *pro* and *con* respecting the result of this astounding expedition—success or failure—the Imperial sceptre once more—or a traitor's grave. During the early part of the voyage, our conversation in the cuddy turned almost exclusively on this absorbing topic: at last, everything connected with the subject having been pretty well exhausted, it was abandoned, about the time we reached the Line, by common consent; after the captain, a gentlemanly man named Crabbe, and myself, had made a bet of a Champagne dinner when we reached Calcutta, respecting the issue of Buonaparte's invasion. He betted that Napoleon would not be in Paris except as a prisoner, on the 15th of April. The dinner was to include all the cabin passengers.

We sailed in a fleet of five ships—all Indiamen—our captain being commodore. One of the ships—the *Princess Charlotte*—the fastest sailer, was employed as a lookout frigate, to reconnoitre any suspicious strangers, as we were not quite sure that we might not fall in with an American frigate in our course; ignorant, most probably, of the Treaty of Ghent that had just been concluded. All the ships had troops on board, and we were determined to make a good fight. We had beautiful weather the whole way; and so fair was the wind, that we had not occasion to wear or tack the whole voyage from the Downs to Madras. We bounded across the Bay of Biscay in fine style, and on the 18th April were off Madeira, but did not stop, for the commodore would not run any risk of parting with his favourable breeze; so we only got a peep through a glass at Funchal. As we moved southward, the sun made us doff our woollens quickly enough. We passed our time agreeably—Captain Crabbe had a respectable library, and he civilly invited us all to enjoy ourselves with a book in his commodious cabin when we pleased. Gazing—strolling on deck—reading and chess, occupied the forenoon; and we generally had whist in the evening.

There was but one drawback to our comfort on board—the irregular conduct of Lieut. L——b——t of our corps. This was a talented young man—most agreeable when sober, but half mad when excited by wine. One night when passing Madeira, L——b——t came out of the cuddy tipsy, knocked down the seaman at the wheel and took his place. The captain was inside; but finding the ship making a wide yaw out of her course, he came running out to see what was the matter; when the new steersman explained—averring that the blockhead he had just ousted knew nothing whatever about his work. This prank was forgiven, and the man got hush-money; but on an exactly similar outrage again occurring—Mr. L——b——t was put under close arrest.

This young man was clever and well read; and, it appeared, had been first spoiled by the sentimental and sensual sophistries of the French philosophic school—chiefly of Rousseau. He considered the *Heloise* the very perfection of eloquence; and that mischievous romance and Lord Byron's *Corsair*, generally lay under his pillow. Numerous were the scrapes in which he involved himself during the Peninsular Campaigns by his intemperance; and manifold were the dangers he ran of losing his commission with disgrace. As some persons can sleep at will, L——b——t possessed the power of sobering himself on a great emergency; so that he always managed to avoid any fatal display of incapacity to do his duty.

When once on an outlying picket before Bayonne, the night after the Second Division crossed the Nive, he got quite drunk and fell asleep. Immediately after, poor Clitheroe, who was afterwards killed at Garris, arrived at the post, with an order to *patrole* in a particular direction in front. I happened to be in the hut at the time—the night was dark and wet, and L——b——t so wrapped in drunken sleep that he could not be wakened, and I thought he was lost. All this time Capt. Clitheroe was waiting at the door for the officer in command of the picket, to give him his instructions. After several attempts I roused him at last, by plunging a large pin up to its head in the calf of his leg—when he started up—rubbed his eyes and his leg—cursed the insect that had bit him—went out and received the *aide-de-camp's* orders—took his picket in the proper direction—patrolled where he was desired, and made a very satisfactory report.

Before we left Chatham, L——b——t sallied out of the Mitre Inn one evening after dinner, with a white-hot poker in his hand. It was Saturday night, and very wet; yet many people were in the streets, and as he proceeded, upsetting everybody he met, winding his formidable weapon—fizzing with the rain—over his head, and spouting German, he looked something like a demon wreathed in fire and smoke.

As we approached the Line we met with the usual number of porpoises, flying fish and sharks. The last being a fish I had not yet enjoyed the pleasure of catching, I baited a hook with a piece of pork, attached this to a chain a foot and a half long, fastened to a strong cord, and promised, a shilling for the first intimation when one of these voracious rascals made his appearance; which was generally in the ship's wake, and very early in the morning.

Two mornings after these arrangements, a sailor shook my cot a little after daylight to announce the arrival of the enemy. I started up and ascended to the poop; and there plain enough, was a good sized shark visible, about three feet below the surface, and four or five yards astern. Over went my bait immediately, and I was delighted to perceive that it was not long unnoticed: the shark came up to the pork, reconnoitred it a little with some attention, poked it with his snout; and then—being satisfied that it was sweet, he turned himself half round, opened his huge mouth and sucked it in. I kindly permitted him to indulge in one squeeze of the luscious morsel, and then, just as he was getting into his former sailing order—chuck went the barb into his jaws.

At first he did not appear to comprehend the meaning of this prick; perhaps supposing it was nothing more than a sharp bit of bone in the pork—but when he found the hook piercing deeper and deeper, and "the iron entering his soul"—down he plunged desperately; but in the meantime the sailors had attached the cord to a coil of rope, and I let him run out as much as he pleased, and then played him like a salmon. By this time half the passengers were up, witnessing the sport. When the shark was fairly tired, I brought him near the surface—a sailor cast a noose adroitly round his body below the pectoral fins—a loud *yo-he-oh!* was sung out by the captors, and we hoisted the gentleman on deck. He there made great play about our legs; but his tail was soon nicked with an axe—the sailors dragged him forward to the cooking galley—cut him up and ate him.

In the warm latitudes we caught a number of *bonitos*, from the bowsprit, with a piece of rag resembling a flying-fish, on which they feed. The *bonito*, notwithstanding its name, is very ugly; and the Portuguese who first named it, could have had little ichthyological taste. Its flesh is very coarse—and only eatable when dressed with some rich sauce, or stewed in wine.

Of course, Neptune did not fail to visit us in crossing the Line, and we had the usual saturnalia. We basked and gasped four or five days becalmed in his dominions; and I know few things so utterly intolerable as to be thus roasted in this burning zone, without the power of leaving it—the pitch starting from the seams of the deck—the perspiration dissolving everything soluble about our clothes, and our very eyeballs straining their moorings. At last one day, when

——'twas sad as sad could be,
And we did speak only to break
The silence of the sea.

All in a hot and copper sky,
The bloody sun at noon
Right up above the mast did stand

No bigger than the moon.

Some sharp-sighted person perceived at a great distance, a small ripple—technically called a cat's paw, on the surface of the mirror-like ocean. All glasses were immediately pointed at it, and we had soon the pleasure of seeing it ruffling and expanding beneath a gentle air, which soon became a respectable breeze. Every inch of canvas was instantly spread, and every mouth opened to inhale the grateful coolness. Soon the gallant ship felt its influence—the white foam was dashed aside from the prow, and we proceeded merrily south.

We had fine weather and an unusually smooth sea going round the Cape, and through the Mozambique channel. When we were abreast of the Island of Johanna, we saw a number of canoes waiting to board us, full of the most grotesquely dressed black figures, apparently arrayed in cast-off English naval and military uniforms; shouting to us to lay-to and throw them a rope. But the commodore was deaf to their entreaties—the wind was too fair to stop even for a levee of Admirals and Generals; and thus the Prince of Wales and the Duke of York and Lord Nelson—till hard-working Arab washermen—lost their job.

Beautiful at this time were the sky above, and the sea below—the one glorious with southern constellations, new to our eyes—the other radiant at night, in our wake, like a river of fire. Philosophers, I humbly think, are at fault in attempting to explain this phenomenon. The phosphorescence of the *molluscae* can scarcely be sufficient; unless we suppose these creatures to be as numerous as the drops of water. May not one universal and simple cause suffice—the collision against each other of particles of briny fluid—charged in warm latitudes with the phosphoric salts—by the violent motion of the ship?

On the 2nd of July we got amongst a large covey of flying-fish—chased by innumerable dolphins and *bonetos*; some of which poor unfortunates jumped into the chains, and even on deck, where they were soon secured. They are extremely delicate eating; tasting much like whiting. This morning I caught a very large shark—being the thirteenth—fully twelve feet long, and weighing one hundred and fifty pounds. This monster gave us an hour's play, and I found my hands all blistered afterwards from the running out and hauling the rope—though quite unconscious of hurt at the time.

Whilst rapidly traversing the Indian Ocean, many and various were our conjectures on board concerning the *res gestae* in Europe; for here there was a full scope for speculation. Leaving England as Napoleon reached Lyons, yet, when the "Bravest of the Brave" was pledged to destroy him, it was hard to say what the event would be. For my own part I entertained little doubt of the general defection of the army; knowing their invincible attachment to their old master, and the electric effect of the first example: and under this impression betted the dinner, which probably would cost a hundred pounds in expensive Calcutta.

On the 17th July we saw Ceylon on our larboard bow; and soon perceived the peculiar odour of land—notwithstanding the groves of cinnamon and spice, certainly more earthy and warm than fragrant. On the 22nd we anchored in Madras Roads.

And now all was intense anxiety to learn the news from Europe, which would be received here up to a late date by an overland despatch. Soon after dropping anchor we saw a *Mussoolah* boat approach with a white face in it; and before the owner had time to board us he was hailed from the gangway—"Any Europe news?"

"Great news" was the reply. But he proceeded leisurely up the ladder and stepped on the quarterdeck before he would tell us anymore. Then, after shaking hands with Captain Crabbe, he satisfied our eager curiosity in three words—"Buonaparte is reigning in the Thuilleries!"

On the 24th we disembarked; and had the novel excitement previously of passing through the Madras surf. Our course was through three successive tiers of foaming and thundering breakers, often looking down upon us as we sat in the bottom of the deep and elastic *Mussoolah* boat; the line of the bottom of which, as we ascended and descended the steep and awful hills of surf, was within a very little of being absolutely perpendicular, and as if it was poised on one end. We were flanked on both sides by a fleet of Catamarans; the inmates of which had various shining medals about their necks, as rewards for saving poor fellows like us from the sharks. *Allah! Allah! Allah!* vociferated the boatmen, as the boat rode over the foaming ridges—*Allah! Allah!* shouted with equal fear and fervency. At last the flood of the third surf shot us up the beach; when a hundred Orientals seizing the boat, for fear of the reflux, dragged us out of the reach of the wave, and we jumped out on the soil of Hindostan.

CHAPTER 23

Voyage up the Ganges.

Man is the only growth that dwindles here.
Goldsmith.

——*the cypress and myrtle*
Are emblems of deeds that are done in their clime.
Bride of Abydos.

Here, then, were we fairly landed in this "Clime of the Sun." My brother officers and myself were immediately assailed by an army of black and yellow and straw-coloured and mud-coloured and many-coloured natives, in large turbans, fine moustaches, earnest faces, long, white, flowing garments, and naked feet, presenting numerous credentials and certificates with low and graceful *salaams*; and requesting to have the high honour of being the humblest of our slaves. With some difficulty we made our way through this crowd, but not before choosing one or two each from this importunate crowd. We then got into *palanquins* and went to the principal hotel.

Next morning we marched to Poonamalee, a military station fifteen miles from Madras; the appearance and *agremens* of which did not prepossess us much in favour of the new country. The barracks were built on a flat; exposed to the heat of a powerful sun—without shade or ventilation: the flies could scarcely have been much worse with Pharaoh, and a sandy plain in front was inhabited by Cobra de Capellos—the most venomous snake in the East. These creatures remained in their holes during the day; but, as soon as it was dark, they sallied out to take a snap at any body's heels that passed. When obliged to pass over this plain during my night visits to the hospital, I was at first very apprehensive of a bite, but I took good care to fortify everything below the knees with as many pairs of boots as I could move in; and thus defied the snakes, although I sometimes fancied I felt the villains tugging at the leather.

After a fortnight at Poonamalee we were ordered to re-embark in the same ship for Calcutta. We marched at two o'clock in the morning to avoid the heat—enjoyed several delicious drinks of toddy—the cool juice of the cocoa-nut palm—on the road—launched out into the surf, attended by the Catamaran people—cheated the sharks—once more found ourselves comfortably settled in the *Lord Melville*; and after a pleasant voyage reached Calcutta on the 23rd of August.

This Metropolis of the East has a grand and imposing aspect; and the beauty of the fine houses at the western extremity particularly—surrounded by their richly ornamented and luxurious grounds and gardens, is very striking. The mansions are on a large scale, compared with English dwellings at home; and their deep verandahs and balconies, with the white *marmorean chunam* with which the walls are covered, give them quite an air of splendour und magnificence.

But to a *Griffin* (as strangers are called) perhaps the greatest novelty in Calcutta is that huge, grave, Dominie Sampson of birds—the adjutant; stalking slowly and formally through the streets—flying round a corner within a yard of your person, with his enormous bill projecting formidably, and threatening you with impalement if you should come in contact with him—gobbling up large bones of beef, or any other trifle he meets, or, when his meal is over, standing like a statue on the highest pinnacle he can find.

The adjutant is a harmless and useful bird, that performs the duty of a scavenger in India—devouring offal, and punishing snakes—of which he is very fond. His valuable services are so fully appreciated, that the Company have taken him into their charge and placed his whole fraternity under their protection—punishing with a heavy fine the murder of one of these birds. Yet, such is the ingratitude of mankind, that the poor inoffensive adjutant is persecuted by the most annoying and cruel tricks. Shank bones of mutton are cleaned out and stuffed with gunpowder, with a slow match applied—then the meat is thrown out and swallowed, and when the poor wretch is chuckling over his savoury morsel, it explodes and blows him to atoms.

A more venial trick—and not unamusing, I confess—is to tie two legs of mutton together with a piece of whip-cord, leaving an interval of three or four yards—the *jigôts* are then tossed out amongst the adjutants, and soon find their way into the stomachs of a couple of the most active of the birds. As long as they keep together it is all very well; but as soon as the cord tightens, both become alarmed and take wing—mutually astonished at the phenomenon, no doubt. A laughable tugging match then ensues in the air—each adjutant striving to mount higher than the other, till at last they attain a great elevation. When at length the weaker bird is forced to disgorge his mutton, a new power comes into play—the force of gravity—and the pendulum leg of mutton brings the conqueror down to the earth a great deal faster than he wishes.

These creatures have prodigious powers of deglutition and digestion. It is a very common thing for one of them to seize an impertinent crow who is troublesome, when the adjutant wants to eat his breakfast in quiet, and after turning him right about face by a skilful *coup de bec*, to send him cawing down his capacious throat. I recollect at Dinapore, when we shook a bag-fox, and had an hour's run one morning, some silly servant brought the dead animal home, and tossed him into the barrack-square amongst the adjutants, who all came flocking about the poor defunct. One ravenous fellow would seize him by the brush—another by the leg—a third by the back—still it would not do—none could manage to gulp him down. At last one large bird set about the business scientifically, and took the fox's head in his mouth; which, after a little straining, was bolted—then, with a great effort he swallowed the body, till nothing remained but a bit of the tail sticking out of his beak. At this the others began to pick; till the gormandizer becoming annoyed at their teasing, flew off with his delicate lunch to digest it at his leisure.

As I feared at the time that this fact, every circumstance of which had passed under my own eyes, would not be credited at home, I called out two of my brother-officers from their breakfasts, to be corroborating evidence. Still, it must rest on my single authority; as poor L'Estrange left his bones at Sierra Leone, and Harvey is also no longer in the land of the living. But no old Indian will doubt the story.

On reaching Calcutta we found that our regiment had left the Presidency for Dinapore, about a fortnight before our arrival. We got quarters in Fort William. At this time the Governor was absent, and everybody was complaining of the stupidity of Calcutta. We saw few except our immediate military superiors; and the only large dinner we partook of in the city of palaces, was the bet dinner at Captain Crabbe's house in Chouringhee.

In the middle of September we embarked on the Hoogly—the westernmost and deepest branch of the Ganges, for Dinapore. Another officer and myself engaged a *budgerow* of sixteen dandies, as they call boatmen in India—and we all formed a mess, and took a native purveyor with us, who engaged to provide us food on the voyage at a very moderate rate. Three other large detachments for different Indian Regiments accompanied us, and I was appointed superintendant *medico* of the whole. In those Saturnian days, John Company paid his doctors well. I received so many *annas* each per head, for the individuals under my charge, including myself; and thus was furnished with an additional reason, value about sixpence a-day, for preserving my own health.

Our voyage up the Ganges was quite a pleasure trip. When the wind was fair, we sailed gallantly against the current; but otherwise we were pulled along the shore by our boatmen, who moved in the water like amphibious animals, totally fearless as to the alligators. At these times I was generally out with my gun, ranging a little into the interior; with a couple of servants and a skiff to observe and follow my motions. In the middle of the day I was always on board attending to the sick. We generally halted for the night at some pleasant spot on the bank, ordinarily near some tope or mango grove. Innumerable were the individual teal, widgeon, mallard, *et id genus omne*, that I shot on this voyage; and whenever there were marshes we were sure to find snipes.

But the resplendent wild peacock! What *can* be a nobler sight than a fine cock, with his two yards of tail, flying over your head: his brilliant plumage nearly dazzling you blind, as the rays of an Indian Sun are reflected from it? And what a sensation when you knock him over. I shot only a few of these magnificent birds, for they are getting scarce in the neighbourhood of the river; and there is an ugly association with them, that has some tendency to spoil one's enjoyment in pursuing them. The peacock jungles are very frequently the haunts of tigers.

The jackals used to annoy us much in ascending the Ganges, by their doleful howling at night. These animals appear to take an odd pleasure in continually disturbing people's repose. There, by moonlight, when I got up, and could no longer bear the noise, would I see a herd of them baying at the boats, until a shot dispersed them. They are harmless creatures, however, and when tamed early, are capable of canine attachment.

Who is there that is not to some extent, skilled in animal physiognomy? A sagacious shepherd will distinguish the face, even, of a sheep from its fellow, amongst a numerous flock: and every one can descry good humour, or sulk, or savageness, in the more intelligent countenance of a dog or a horse. Whilst in India, I paid some attention to the expression of elephants' and buffaloes' faces—the latter a very rugged and unpromising study. For, I believe, of all the tamed animals, except the camel, the buffalo is the most ugly and unprepossessing.

During one of my rambles on this voyage, I passed a buffalo bull in a field; but, observing something peculiarly treacherous in his whole appearance, I cocked both barrels, and prepared for mischief; and well it was that I had critically noticed the expression of his savage eye: for I had not advanced from him thirty paces, when he charged me with a roar. I stood firm, and when he came so near that missing him was impossible, he had the benefit of a barrel in each eye. The pain maddened the blinded brute; and, ferocious monster as he was, I could scarcely help feeling pity when I saw him roaring with agony and revolving in a bloody circle: and though his infamous conduct scarcely deserved the act of mercy, I put a ball in each barrel and killed him. My two native servants had scampered off very valiantly when they saw the beast attacking me but when they found him shot, there was no end to their compliments to *saahib* on the occasion.

On these little expeditions, it was amusing to observe the absurd fear the Indian domestic cattle shew of a white man: snorting at his approach—throwing up their noses and running out of his way with all speed. One day when in quest of partridges, I happened to jump into a lane, and there confronted a Hindu riding on one of his gods—a Brahminee Bull, who carried besides two bags of rice. On perceiving my white face, the animal bolted to the right about so suddenly that he unshipped his Indian master, bags of paddy and all, and ran snorting up the lane in a state of great alarm. The Indian, after pulling his bags out of the dirt, ran to catch his deity; whom he abused in the grossest manner his very gross and copious language would permit.

We continued our voyage prosperously and pleasantly. The troops were healthy, notwithstanding the horrid habits of intemperance which the ardent climate and cheap spirits engender. We reached Dinapore on the 2nd November, and I delivered my charge all safe and sound; no casualty having occurred in the detachment since we left the Isle of Wight.

CHAPTER 24

Camp

Evening comes on: arising from the stream
Homeward the tall Flamingo wings his flight;
And where he sails athwart the setting beam
His scarlet plumage glows with deeper light.

Southey.

The 66th Regiment marched from Dinapore in the direction of the Nepaul Hills, the very day we arrived. These hills and the intervening Ghoorkah Valleys, lie at the base of those stupendous mountains, the Himalayan Chain, whose white tops we could clearly see, though two hundred miles off, at a considerable elevation above the horizon, looking like stationary clouds. Things were beginning to look warlike in that quarter—the *Rajah* of Nepaul demurred at ratifying the treaty of peace which had been signed by his Minister: a force was about to be assembled to coerce him, and a camp had been traced out on the frontier. On our arrival we found that the sick, the women and children, heavy baggage, &c., had been left here—I was directed to remain till farther orders, but a hint was given to equip for a campaign.

Thus far into the bowels of the land I had come prosperously, and now was about to contrast Indian with European warfare, and to exchange the pretty valleys of the Pyrenees for the stupendous sublimities of the Himalaya Mountains. My domestic establishment expanded something in the same ratio. I had my *surdar*-bearer, supposed to be honest, *par excellence*; and bound by every honourable tie to let nobody cheat me but himself:—nine common bearers for my *palanquin*—two *chohkhedars* or watchmen—my *dhoby* or water-carrier—my *dhurjee* or tailor—my *khitmugar*—my *mnausalgee*, the *syce* and his assistant to take care of my horse—three men to look after the bullocks—some others, whose duties I forget: and my incomparable Bastee Rhamm, with resplendent, jet-black moustaches, curling like the horns of his namesake, to superintend my *hookah*.

O Antonio, my faithful valet, and thou hard-fisted Jonathan Wild, my trusty groom! often did I regret you, when groaning in the splendid bondage of being lord over twenty and nine bedizened, and bemuslined, and sashed, and slashed, and slippered, and turbaned attendants.

It is the custom in India for strangers to call on the residents on their first arrival—the visit is soon returned, and an invitation follows; for in that part of the world the exercise of hospitality is more a luxury than a virtue, and breaking the monotony of one's isolation in a remote part of the country, and staying a day or two, is, in fact, a favour conferred on the host. About a week after my arrival, I went to dine with the Collector of the District, who lived at Patna. I was rather early, and nobody was in the drawing-room when I entered. We had been quite in the dark, as to European news, since we left Madras: by the last accounts, enormous preparations were making by the Allies, and corresponding exertions by Napoleon—the Duke of Wellington had gone to Flanders, and Blucher was assembling the Prussians. I knew that these two men would do all that skill and energy could accomplish. But then, on the other hand, the flower of the British Regiments not yet returned from America—the short time—the second battalions—the young soldiers—the doubtful Belgians—contrasted with the unity of Buonaparte's operations, and the desperate bravery to be expected from his officers and soldiers. As these gloomy ideas were passing through my mind, in looking out of one of the windows, I turned, almost mechanically, to divert them, towards some prints on a table; on the top of which lay a Calcutta newspaper, at which I cast a hasty glance. It contained the Duke of Wellington's *Despatch of the Battle of Waterloo!*

We dined, but I could think of nothing but the defence of Hougoumont, and the glorious and invincible squares, and the charges of the *Cuirassiers*, and the death of Picton and Ponsonby, and humbler names whom I had known in the Peninsula—and the mowing down of the French cavalry, and the final and irrecoverable rout, and the meeting of Wellington and Blucher! The good host saw my absence of mind, but divined the cause. I was absolutely drunk with joy.

I marched on the 9th December, with another officer of the regiment, for the camp in the *terraie*, as the belt of level land round the base of the first hills is called. We crossed the Ganges near Dinapore, and at once got into a fertile and populous country. Our marches were only ten miles a-day; the weather was cool and clear. Latitude, about thirty degrees north; and altogether the journey was more a pleasant shooting expedition than a march. We always breakfasted early, and sent on our baggage, with directions to encamp ten miles off, in the most convenient tope the servants could find, and then set about cooking our dinner; whilst we kept a couple of horses and attendants, and digressed from the road whenever we found game.

On the third day, we had accumulated such a quantity that we were embarrassed with our riches—but, fortunately, meeting some Company's officers, known to my companion, we begged they would assist us in our distress. Our cook set to work, and having bruised the heads of sixty or seventy couple of snipe, they were put into a kettle to make soup, with a few brace of partridges, and a number of *ortolans*, that we met in flocks every day. I don't know the exact gastronomic name our soup was entitled to, but this I know, that it was exquisitely good. The rest of the game dinner was in harmony.

The next day we had again good sport; having entered a country irrigated by numerous artificial ponds and tanks, to which vast numbers of water-fowl resorted. In the evening we found our tents pitched in a mango *tope*, with turf as smooth as velvet, by the side of a considerable lake. It was near sunset, and we were about to dress for dinner, when I saw a wild peacock emerging from the jungle, fifty yards from the water, and running down to drink opposite our tents. I seized my gun, went down the pond a little way, got across in an old canoe, and then commenced the delicate operation of turning his flank: diving into the jungle, and at the expense of some scratches, getting quite in his rear, and cutting him off from his cover.

I then advanced until about thirty yards distant; whilst the vain bird, after satisfying his thirst, appeared inclined to pick a quarrel with his image in the clear water. He received one barrel before he took flight, without much apparent injury; for these strong birds are so mailed by their thick feathers that they require large shot, at a short distance, to kill them and I could hear my charge rattling on his quills, without preventing his getting up vigorously. The reserve artillery, however, brought him down with a broken wing; and even then he nearly escaped into the jungle before I caught him, when he made a desperate fight. I presented this bird to the Mess the day of our arrival in camp. It was buried in moist earth five days, after which the flesh was tender, and of fine flavour.

We found a large encampment near the hamlet of Bulwee; consisting of three British regiments, the 24th, 87th and ours, with twelve or thirteen battalions of *sepoys* and artillery; the whole commanded by Sir David Ochterlony. Our camp enjoyed a splendid view of the mountains; and though we had come a hundred miles nearer, there was not much difference between the appearance of their dazzling summits here, and at Dinapore. Our position was only six miles from a belt of jungle at the foot of the first range of hills, that was full of wild animals.

To one just arrived, after campaigning in Europe, the novelty and luxury of an Indian camp were extremely pleasing and amusing. There was a large and heterogeneous host of followers—about twenty for every soldier—consisting of the *bazaar* people, *coolies*, *bangywallies*, jugglers, *nautch* girls—offcers' and soldiers' servants—tent-people; and attendants on the numerous public elephants, camels and bullocks. We had a good *bazaar*, and plenty of provisions; and as one proof of the goodness of our fare, I may mention that at the Mess we had green peas in abundance, that had been carried in baskets on men's shoulders from Dinapore.

Here we remained six weeks, whilst negotiations were going on with the Ghoorkahs. Our last campaign against them had been on the whole, unsuccessful; and some failures in attempts on their forts and other untoward affairs, had given them confidence. We were now under arms at daylight every morning, but after this parade we had the day to ourselves: and as this was a rich and new country for the sportsman, we had plenty of amusement; fox and jackal hunting and coursing, and abundance of snipe—common and painted—with great variety of waterfowl. A tiger, even, would now and then leave his lair in the jungle, to pay us a visit, and one large fellow had been seen in the neighbourhood of the camp three or four times. At length Dr. Richardson, of the Company's Service, a celebrated tiger-hunter, determined to go in quest of him; and having heard that I was very anxious for an opportunity of getting a shot, he was kind enough to offer me a seat on his elephant.

We started for a ravine, four miles from camp, whither the brute had been recently tracked; mounted on a steady and trained male elephant, with a pair of magnificent tusks, fit to transfix any tiger in the forest. I had my own double gun, and a rifle which my friend lent me.

Behold me then at last; peaceful son of Æsculapius though I was—arrived at the very *acme* of my ambition in the sporting line—every nerve and muscle high strung—every mental and bodily power screwed to the utmost tension for the approaching collision.

We were not long in discovering the enemy's retreat; but he slunk away before we could get a shot within proper distance, and we beat about the whole day without success. The same bad luck also attended us on our second expedition; but we were determined to try once more, and skirted the jungle to a great distance without seeing anything larger than a black partridge. As we were returning in bad spirits at our ill fortune, in passing through a low brake, two miles from camp, the elephant became excited, threw up his trunk and made a dead point. In five minutes afterwards the noble game we were in quest of, gave an angry growl as he emerged from a bush, not ten yards in front of us, and slowly got out of our way. We were both cool, for all our energies had been exerted to preserve presence of mind; so that we fired with certain aim, and in four seconds as many balls struck the tiger. He roared horribly—lashed his sides—turned and attempted to spring at us, but failed, for a fore leg had been broken. Three more balls despatched him: and after pausing until we saw all motion cease, we alighted, cautiously approached, and stood over our fallen enemy.

There are bright but evanescent periods in our lives, when we feel the blood circulating in our veins as if it was charged with electricity; (which it literally may be), when each pulse is full of tenfold power and vitality—when we feel so vividly the presence of our immaterial nature that we conceive we could triumph over all gross mundane obstacles, and carry every volition into instant execution. Something like this proud consciousness of power animated us when we saw this tremendous tyrant of the forest lying extended at our feet—yet grim and dreadful even in death.

We entered the camp with our glorious prize. The tiger was a noble male of the very largest size—ten feet four inches from nose to tail. I measured his fore leg near the shoulder, with my pocket handkerchief, and found it exactly the same circumference as my own body under the arms; which is somewhat above medium size. Every muscle of the limb was as defined and as hard as a cord of iron.

The elephants and camels of our little army, were picketed near the part of the camp occupied by our regiment. One refractory brute amongst the former, was beginning to shew dangerous symptoms of ferocity, calling for suitable treatment; and severe enough was the discipline he received. They chained him by the four legs to a large tree, which even *his* power could scarcely shake—half-starved him for a week, and every morning they pricked him with half a dozen long bamboos, armed with sharp spikes, about the neck and roots of the ears; when the animal's violent exertions would make the blood spout out frightfully. In this way they brought him to his senses, and he was quiet enough in about ten days.

Had Mr. Cross of Exeter Change, adopted some such plan, he might have saved Chuny's life. I recollect in 1822, taking two young ladies to see the wild beasts; when I noticed that Chuny looked wicked, and recommended that he should be forthwith bled and treated after the Indian fashion. But it appeared that Mr. Cross wished to treat and physic his elephant according to the Hamiltonian system, and trust exclusively to drastic doses. The keeper told me that the quantities ordered, were—after a day's fast—four ounces of calomel in a sugar bolus—*hora somni;* and eight and twenty pounds of Epsom salts, disguised in a tub of treacle, on getting out of bed in the morning.

There chanced to be a female elephant and her calf stationed not far from my tent. I carried the young one a large basin of sweet tea, after breakfast one morning; into which he dipped his trunk and drained the contents in an instant; and, perceiving his mamma looking on wistfully, I procured her one also, which she drank with much gusto. Soon after this introduction we became great friends, and the mother and her son were regular pensioners of my teapot: the lady permitting me to take many liberties with her person; such as toying with her delicate ear, scratching her neck, &c., and giving me now and then a hug about the waist with her trunk, which in no instance exceeded the reasonable bounds of a friendly embrace. One morning when she was particularly affectionate, I took a fancy to feel her pulse, and when handling her ear, I groped for an artery at the base, and noted the number of pulsations in a minute; which was twenty-four—and I need scarcely add that there was no want of strength.

By the end of January 1816, matters began to assume a more warlike aspect in the camp. Preparations wore begun for an invasion of the enemy's sequestered valleys—the sick were sent to the rear—heavy artillery and more troops arrived in camp—the whole force, consisting of seventeen thousand men, was formed into four Divisions—one of which, consisting of our own regiment, nine hundred strong, and four *sepoy* battalions, was placed under the command of our excellent commanding officer, Colonel Nicol. His column was destined to penetrate into the Nepaul valley by the Bicknee; or most western Pass, whilst the other columns were to pierce the formidable frontier of mountain and forest, by three other goat-paths, dignified with the name of Passes, simultaneously with ourselves.

On the 4th of February we broke up our camp, and marched westward, skirting the mountain to Rhamnahgur, the residence of a *rajah*. All the *terraie* in this neighbourhood appeared well cultivated, and the soil good; whilst the vicinity of the huge snowy mountains maintained a freshness and coolness of climate which was very agreeable. Our mornings were sometimes cold—the thermometer standing at 36° of Fahrenheit, and at mid-day up to 76 or 80°. But the whole country is dreadfully unhealthy in the hot weather.

On the 14th February we arrived opposite the entrance of the Pass, whore stood a Hindoo Temple of great sanctity, on a hill called Maahur a Jaggra, which was deserted by the Brahmins on our approach. It was covered with the usual emblems of the worship of the Lingam. The view of the mountain Pass we were about to enter, seen from the top of this temple, was magnificent. Two days were spent in fortifying this strong hill, as a point of importance in preserving our communications with the rear; and three hundred *sepoys* and two guns were left as a garrison. These arrangements being made, and our Commissariat stores well up, we prepared for a dash through the belt of forest, and an invasion of the Nepaul territory. We had seen no person—the spies could give us no certain intelligence—except the scream of the parroquet, all was silent in the deep forest around us: and this ominous calm, whilst it impressed the weaker spirits with an undefined dread of something terrible, cheered the bolder with the confidence of certain success.

CHAPTER 25

Superb Order and Fine Strength of the 66th Regiment

Majestic woods of every vigorous green,
Stage above stage, high waving o'er the hills,
Or to the far horizon wide diffused;
A boundless, deep immensity of shade.

Thompson

On the 17th of February, the column of Colonel Nicol entered first the enemy's territory. After penetrating through five miles of thick jungle, we came to the mouth of the Bhicknee Pass, which we found commencing in the dry bed of a river, about one hundred and fifty yards wide; with very high steep banks, covered with enormous *saahl* and teak trees, and thick underwood—altogether exceedingly strong and defensible. We, of course, expected opposition here, but saw not a creature, except deer and monkeys: the latter were of a large size, numerous and noisy—running along the tops of the trees on the high banks, parallel with our advance—scolding and gesticulating, and occasionally pelting us with nuts. Like true patriots, they opposed our invasion with all their might.

When we had proceeded five or six miles up the *nullah*, it became all at once very narrow, and the day being well advanced, it was deemed prudent to halt and look about us. Accordingly, the baggage soon came up; for in our present position we could not safely leave it far behind the column, and we pitched our tents as well as we could in the confined water-course, where all was stone, with no earth to hold a peg. Then, having carefully posted treble cordons of pickets in all directions, we proceeded to make our toilet and prepare for dinner.

There was very great desertion amongst the followers of the camp, chiefly the *bazaar* people, on this first day's march in an enemy's country, from apprehension of the Ghoorkah Mountaineers, who had acquired a high warlike name amongst the effeminate Asiatics. Our personal servants, however, continued staunch during the whole campaign. The Mess marquee was soon up, and the dinner was put upon the stocks forthwith. And, *certes*, it was no small enjoyment to sit down in those wild solitudes, not merely to a good, but a luxurious dinner, with our wine cooled artificially, in an absolute, literal "wilderness of monkeys," chattering high above our heads, and surrounded by beasts of prey: liable too, to be washed off, *en masse*, by any accidental thunderstorm in the mountains. For the river, that now lent us its dry bed for a couch, and was kind enough to trickle between the large stones in a stream scarcely perceptible, but still sufficient to water man and beast, might, in an hour or two, save the Ghoorkahs a world of trouble.

Next day our *nullah* fairly ended in a *cul-de-sac*, and after exploring in all directions, the quarter master general could find nothing but a faint and doubtful sheep track: yet, this was all the high road that the country furnished; consequently we set to work to enlarge it for the passage of the artillery. The bearings of our route being known, the pioneers began to hew and burn, clearing their way through the primeval forest, guided only by the compass and the sun. And now the scene was grand—the fire and the axe opening us a path into the enemy's country, and glorious trees, a hundred and fifty feet high, were seen spouting out huge pyramids of flame before us, the beacons of our advance, whilst a touch of the grotesque was added to the sublime by the utter alarm and consternation of the great white-faced baboons with which they were peopled.

Still we saw not a human being, and our Light Companies, that threaded the forest on the flanks of the column, met with no opposition but the formidable jungle through which they were slowly penetrating. This was strange, considering the nature of the defile we were passing through; and many began to entertain fears that a still stronger pass yet awaited us; and that the Ghoorkahs were preparing certain Claudine forks for Brigadier Nicol, although not deeply acquainted with Roman story.

For four days we proceeded thus through forest and *nullah*, cuttings a rough carriage road as we went on, and feeling our way cautiously, but no enemy appeared. The chief inconvenience we experienced was from the round stones in the dry water-courses, which got between the clefts of the hoof and lamed our bullocks. The elephants stood this better; their thick-soled and elastic boots bearing their weight over pebbles as well as anything else. On the march I sometimes passed my female friend and her son; and although the eye of these animals looks heavy, I fancied I could notice a twinkle of recognition in the old one's physiognomy, conveying a hint how agreeable it would be if I would send her an invitation to tea some evening.

At length it appeared probable that the sameness of our lumbering advance would be relieved by a little lighting, *pour nous désennuyer*, as positive information was received that a strong stockade had been prepared a little way in our front, whidi the enemy were determined to defend with a large force. Preparations were instantly made to attack it. Flanking detachments were ordered right and left to turn the position, while the artillery were got ready to batter, and a strong column was directed to storm. But when all was ready, we found that the enemy had decamped precipitately; and from this and other circumstances, it was conjectured that there had been fighting on our right, and the more central passes had been forced—consequently our immediate antagonists had retired for fear of being cut off from the road to Khatmandoo, their capital.

As soon as we found that the stockade before us had been abandoned, we pushed on and crossed the highest point of the first range of mountains on the 23rd, after passing through one of the strongest defiles I ever saw, which had been carefully stockaded, and covered with abattis in different places. From the summit we descried a cultivated valley, through which the River Rapté, a clear, winding stream, flowed prettily. The inhabitants had all fled on our arrival. Here we found a small mud-fort near the village of Accoah, where we were obliged to halt two days to rest the cattle.

The Rapté is an auriferous stream, and we picked up some particles of gold as big as small shot. The water was very clear, and abounded in fish, somewhat resembling dace, but of an unknown *genus*. The first evening after our arrival, I caught a couple of dozen as large as herrings, with trout-flies. They were sweet and firm, and afforded a little treat to the Mess.

The morning after entering this valley, I happened to enter the tent of my eccentric friend, L—— b——t, who had annoyed us so much on the voyage out. He was sitting up in bed, with his writing desk on his knees, hard at work; his face much flushed—eyes bloodshot—appearance altogether very wild, and two pistols lying on a camp table beside him. At the first glance, I saw that mischief was impending, but said nothing more than the usual salutations, and sat down. He continued writing for a quarter of an hour, and then addressed me, "Doctor, I am making my will—I have left you my books and my sabre, as mementoes of friendship. Do you see those pistols? examine them—well, you find they are loaded—one is destined for Colonel Nicol—a ball from the other will finish my own career—you are shocked—you will remonstrate in vain, my purpose is irrevocable."

It was necessary to temporize; so I listened quietly and pretended to enter into the story of his griefs, and even to go farther, and affect some sympathy with them. I learned that the origin of the matter was this. At the Battle of Vittoria, when General Byng's Brigade was ordered to lie down behind a small hill, to secure themselves from a heavy cannonade, at the beginning of the action L——b——t sillily jumped up and ran to the top, posting himself on an elevated point— thus drawing fire on himself and those in the rear. When Colonel Nicol observed this he cried out, "come down Sir, instantly—this needless exposure is an act of madness, not a proof of courage." These words had rankled in his mind ever since, and now, in his drunken delirium, he was preparing to take a fatal revenge for the insult.

It was of course necessary to take some decided step, but not so easy to fix on what was to be done: after a little reflection, I decided on my course. "My dear fellow," I said, "your hand shakes so much this morning, and your eyes are so much inflamed, that you could not hit a church at ten paces—still less a man—your head too, must ache confoundedly after that rascally wine last night—let me feel your pulse—hah—your tongue- foul—fever, by Jove—brain fever! loss of mind soon—perhaps before tomorrow morning—come, come, this will never do—call your servant—a basin instantly—your master must be bled."

From various circumstances, including former professional services, I had acquired much influence over L——b——t, and I needed it all now, for he was very refractory; but the point was at last carried. The servant brought in a wash-hand basin—I tied up his arm—opened a vein, and had it spouting, *pleno rivo*, as we say, in a minute. I was not very particular us to the number of ounces, within a dozen or so, but when the basin was nearly full my object was accomplished, and the patient fainted. The pistols, sword, razors, &c., were then secured, and himself close watched till the frenzy was over.

On the 25th of February, we moved up the valley of the Rapté; not having yet seen a human being. But on this march we met three or four natives—broad-faced, hardy-looking Tartars. They told us there had been fighting on the right, and one of the central passes had been stormed. We pushed on as fast as the difficult route would permit, and on the 2nd of March, joined Sir David and the main body of the army, encamped on a plain, at the foot of the mountain of Muckawnpore.

We were much concerned to find that we had come too late to participate in a sharp affair on the mountain, three days before, in which the Ghoorkahs had fought well, but had been beaten with great loss. The enemy had several wooden guns in the action, with iron hoops, and beat-iron balls—one of which had killed the commander in chief's *hurkaru*, close to his side. The Light Company of the 87th had the principal fighting, and had behaved with great gallantry. One of our men had gone up the hill, attached to the 87th, and had done his duty so well, as to cause the commanding officer of that corps, to give him a written certificate of most excellent conduct in the action. I heard him say, when he presented this document to Colonel Nicol, "I was the only 66th man in the field, Sir; so Sir, I thinks I must fight my best—I peppered three of them anyhow. Sir, to a cartainty." It was on this hill that John Shipp, of the 87th, had his celebrated duel with a Ghoorkah Chief. [1]

It was clear that our commander in chief was well pleased at our arrival, for he had only one British Regiment at Headquarters, and the enemy had displayed courage; and a formidable force, and still held the highest and strongest part of the mountain range, where they had built some stockades.

The day after our arrival, fresh operations began. The whole of our regiment, and a grenadier battalion of *sepoys*, with four guns on elephants, were ordered up the hill; with directions to push on cautiously along the ridge, and establish ourselves on a commanding point. I accompanied this brigade. The road up the mountain was only a path—extremely steep; and the *mahouts* had great difficulty in forcing on their elephants, which moaned and groaned indignantly at the unwonted labour of this toilsome ascent. When our whole force was collected, we advanced boldly some way to the eastward, until within about eight hundred yards of the enemy's nearest stockade, when we halted, and entrenched ourselves for the night. Pickets were then placed in advance, and on the flanks of our position, in which

1. *The Extraordinary Military Career of John Shipp* by John Shipp, also published by Leonaur.

eight guns were mounted.

My gallant *hookebadar*, Bastee Rhamm, a fine, tall, soldier-looking man, who was a discharged grenadier *sepoy*, stuck close to my side in going up the hill; wearing his *tulwar*, or short sword, and having a couple of my *hookah* snakes, folded circularly, on his back, after the fashion of a shield. We had a cold dinner, and afterwards, every officer produced his private stock of brandy, and his *cheroot*, or cigar. But the incomparable Bastee Rhamm, who gloried in triumphing over all difficulties in the discharge of his vocation, had by some means, carried the *hookah* to the top of the mountain; and in a trice, the fragrant tube was prepared, the charcoal balls ignited—the silver mouth-piece, wreathed with folds of snow-white muslin, was put in my hand, with the usual graceful *salaam*—the *nicotiana* exhaled its aromatic breath—the cool water bubbled—and I enjoyed as perfect a *chillum* on this wild mountain, as at the Mess Room in Dinapore.

The evening was clear, and we could see the Ghoorkah chieftains reconnoitring us, or walking about under huge umbrellas, borne by their attendants; although the declination of the sun at that time, rendered it quite unnecessary. Some of our people asserted that they could with their glasses, perceive marks of apprehension in their faces—but this was probably fancy. As night fell, our fellows lined the intrenchment around our guns, with fixed bayonets, and the whole force remained under arms until daylight.

And here, a slight allusion to the beautiful condition and efficiency of the 66th regiment on that occasion, and to its uniform good conduct, may not be unsuitable nor ungraceful, as a small tribute for eight and twenty happy years passed in it. From the time of entering the enemy's country, not even one solitary act of misbehaviour had occurred in the corps—there was absolutely nothing to find fault with—all pressed on with alacrity; obeying all orders, and performing all duties with equal cheerfulness. Thus it has ever been the case with the British Army, generally, in the face of danger; and it is a national trait to be proud of, that the same appalling circumstances on flood or field, that paralyse feebler natures, only serve "to screw their courage to the sticking place," figuratively and literally.

But, to resume my slight panegyric—when the order came to mount the hill of Muckawnpore, and take the honourable position of leading regiment in the advance, prepared to storm the enemy's stockades in succession—I never saw soldiers in such magnificent fighting order before or since. Even the eight sick in the hospital tent, sharing the fine feeling of their comrades, and under the influence of martial excitement which extinguished illness—left it in a body, unknown to the surgeon, and joined the regiment on the hill—the only irregularity during the campaign.

It was, then, sitting in the redoubt on the topmost point of the mountain of Muckawnpore, surrounded by nine hundred of these noble fellows with fixed bayonets, that I moralized over my *hookah*, whilst my brother-officers moved about in animated conversation respecting the scene of blood which the morning might witness. There stood the formidable stockade in front, over which the rising moon was slowly climbing, that we were to storm at dawn. And there gleamed around us the array of British bayonets, irradiated by the same yellow orb, by which the fortress was to be won.

After two or three *chillums* amidst such superb associations, I wrapped myself up in my cloak, lay down upon the turf and fell asleep.

Whilst I was comfortably enjoying a sound nap—dreaming, most probably, of amputated arms and legs, or spouting arteries; and when waking visions of glory in the foreground, and a perspective of prize money at Khatmandoo, flitted before the fancies of my brother-officers in the trenches, an event occurred that dissipated all our speculations. The Ghoorkah *rajah*, frightened at our advance, accepted the terms proposed to him, and signed the treaty; and a *vakeel*, bearing the ratified instrument, came in during the night under a flag of truce, and went down to the camp. In passing through our post his attendants repeated in Hindoostanee, the one important word, "Peace!" which our native servants soon brought to our ears. Immediately all was botheration and dismay—intelligence came up from camp that the war was at an end; and in the morning we received orders to abandon our strong hill and join the Army on the plain.

CHAPTER 26

March to Quarters

Thy sword within the scabbard keep
And let mankind agree;
Better the world were fast asleep
Than kept alive by thee
The fools are only thinner
With all our cost and care;
But neither side a winner,
For things are as they were.

Dryden.

Thus, then, were dissipated into thin air all our anticipations of a glorious campaign, the capture of the enemy's capital; and the division amongst the Army of some *crores* of *rupees*. When the news became generally known, I never witnessed such a change, nor mortification and disappointment more vividly painted in human countenances than on the hardy visages of our men. The high tension of feature—the self-confiding look—the beaming of ardent eyes—those presages and pledges of success, had disappeared, and been replaced by a somewhat sullen and reckless indifference.

My own hopes of prize-money had been faint from the beginning; as I could not perceive any satisfactory data to reason on in the calculation of much treasure or valuable property to be met with. The stockades only contained wooden guns, and if there was any treasure at Khatmandoo they would probably carry it off to the mountains, and hide it on our approach. From these considerations, when we were talking over the subject one day at the Mess, and most of the officers appeared very sanguine in their expectations—I offered to sell my share of prize-money for a small sum—fifty *rupees*—I think.

A field-officer took me at my word, and sent me the money the same evening; and thus, a very insignificant personage, was the only officer in the Army that pocketed any prize-money.

On the 8th of March, we began to retrace our steps; and on the first day's march through the central Pass, we saw the huge carcasses of five elephants that had been poisoned on the advance. The Ghoorkahs had infused a plant resembling the Belladonna in a fine spring at the top of the Pass; and the poor animals, thirsty and fatigued after the steep ascent, had drunk freely. Here, their characteristic sagacity was at fault; but these noble creatures could not suspect such villainy in the lords of the creation. When the poison began to take effect, their agonies and groans were frightful; but danger being apprehended from the madness that pain might cause, it became necessary to destroy them, and they were shot.

We halted at Bettiah, the residence of a *rajah*, where we found a Christian Mission from Goa, established nearly fifty years. The priest, whose name was Julius Caesar, was a fine, apostolic-looking man, a Portuguese, apparently learned, and speaking several languages with facility. I found him in the chapel, catechizing the native children, who were numerous. He said his congregation consisted of three hundred individuals. The station is admirably situated for spreading Christianity into the Nepaul valleys—perhaps, ultimately to China; and may in process of time become a missionary position of great importance.

The hot winds set in on our march, which was thus made very disagreeable, as we were involved in clouds of dust nearly the whole way—impelled by a strong gale. We reached Dinapore on the 28th of March.

Here the regiment remained three months. The weather was dreadfully hot; and although we reduced the temperature full twenty degrees, by artificial evaporation from the fragrant grass mats with which our dwellings were surrounded, we could never bring Fahrenheit's Thermometer lower than eighty-eight or ninety degrees. Men were constantly employed in sprinkling water, from the skinful they carried, on the mats; and the first gush of cooled air passing through them into the doors and windows, and carrying with it the freshness and sweet odour of the grass, was very delightful. But the *cuscuss* required constant wetting, and the *bheesties* were apt to be negligent, and then the temperature would become insupportable. There was no moving out of the house, except for an hour in the morning and evening—and all day within, existence was little better than a succession of gasps and gapes.

Our professional duties were performed very early in the morning, and we were invariably at the hospital by sunrise, and there remained busy enough all the cool time, whilst the other officers were taking their invigorating ride. For, now that the excitement and tension of the last short campaign had been followed by languor and relaxation, mental and corporeal, the sick list swelled out marvellously. Thus, our only chance of getting a morning ride occasionally, was for the assistant or surgeon to do the other's duty: and this, at a sickly time, is heavy work—a matter which I very humbly hope the Right Honourable the Secretary at War, for the time being, will take into consideration, previous to the next boon to the medical department.

Perhaps one's breakfast is the only meal *eaten* in India—all the rest are sad piddling work, and merely a form. When I returned from my professional duty, there was—*Primo*—my shave—and I take some credit for having virtuously resisted all temptations here to soapy sloth—for I was always my own barber. *Secundo*, my refreshing shower-bath. *Tertio*, a breakfast of the first order of merit; and *Quarto*, my *hookah*. For, ever watchful at his post, behind my armchair, there stood Bhastee Rhamm, waiting for the close of the meal, to hand "Doctor *Saahib*" the incomparable *chillum*; and to retire, with the usual low *salaam*, to a reverential distance, until the nod of approbation from his master should make him happy. Then were the feet thrown carelessly upon the table—the odoriferous smoke was slowly inhaled, and the ample bowl of Mandarin tea, its morning accompaniment, sipped voluptuously.

After an hour spent thus, the rest of the day, it must be confessed, was heavy in hand. There was no reading attentively without headache—writing involved perspiration to a dissolving extent. Playing backgammon—in addition to the necessity of dry linen every hit or two—burst the tympanum. Playing chess burst the brain. Playing billiards was a labour of Hercules. Thus, were there great difficulties in finding any rational mode of passing the day; and, for want of a better, I thought I might as well fall in love.

There was an English family at Dinapore, with whom I became acquainted. The gentleman commanded a distinguished regiment of Bengal Native Infantry, that had behaved most gallantly in one of the early attacks on Bhurtpore, under Lord Lake—the lady was one of the most pleasing and accomplished women I ever knew. There were two young ladies—one her sister, the other his. The latter, whose name was

174

S——, was the fair object of my affection.

On an impartial retrospect, and after the passion of early years has subsided, and cool judgment has given its verdict respecting the object of it, I am still of the same opinion I was then, that S—— M—— was a very loveable and delightful girl. It is certain that I soon became very fond of her. I by no means wonder that this said inexplicable matter, love, has been so much and so universally lauded in all ages and nations. If it were for no nobler reason than the entire exemption from feeling the little ills and inconveniencies of life which a true passion confers; and the gilding which it sheds upon the homely landscapes around us, it would be deserving of all praise. Truly, as Wordsworth expresses it—who no doubt spoke from experience—

There is a comfort in the strength of love
'Twill make a thing endurable, which else
Would overset the brain——

When I fell in love, I suddenly found myself proof against all the *desagremens* of hot winds, mosquitoes, blue devils, and all that was diabolical in Dinapore. My passion was a conductor through which all atmospherical annoyances and disturbances passed without molestation or injury, after it was once set up. Independent of this subordinate and somewhat selfish consideration, there is no small delight in making yourself agreeable to a pleasing young woman, and in discerning daily new chords and harmonies of feeling, and sentiment, and opinion between her and yourself; and in seeing with your own eyes the growing expansion of little buds of amiability into lovely flowers; not to mention the thought that the sweet bouquet they will make is to be worn in your own bosom.

My friend, Major M——, was a cultivated and gentlemanly, as well as most gallant soldier. He had a very select collection of books, and maintained a handsome establishment. Having been of some professional assistance to one of the family, I gradually became intimate, and at last spent half my time in his house.

Our regiment gave two or three balls on a grand scale at Dinapore, and on the last occasion we covered a large space of the green square opposite the Mess-House with marquee-tents, and laid out a very handsome supper-table there, with a long and tasteful avenue, brilliantly lighted, connecting it with the ballroom. When the ball was over, which was about sunrise, I escorted my fair friend's *palanquin* home, like a trusty *paladin*, after passing an enchanting evening; for I can designate it by no fitter term.

The day after our party was the hottest I ever felt, and quite calm; so that we derived little benefit from our fragrant *cuscuss* envelopes, which hung uselessly at our doors and windows, without a breath of air to rob them of their moisture. After passing a couple of hours at the M———s, I went to the Mess to dinner, which was, as usual, a very good one, but no dish was touched, except the Mulligatawny Soup, of which one or two partook. I came home early and went to bed; but the house was too hot for any repose, even after the dancing of the night before. The evening was still as calm as the day had been: thinking, therefore, that my only chance of a nap was in the open air, I made my servants carry out my couch into the square in front of the door, and wrap me round carefully with the mosquito curtains. In this position I soon fell fast asleep.

Dreams are immaterial miracles; still they cause no wonder: yet, if we were to dream but once in our lives, we would take good care, like Sultan Tippoo, to record our vision. How can they be satisfactorily explained? The spiritual part acts with surprising energy, we know; but whence is it that one faculty only works, whilst the rest are as powerless and torpid as the body they inhabit? By what strange emancipation are the fetters which Judgement throws over Imagination shaken off, and that fantastic sprite allowed to wing her way into worlds of her own, and to revel amidst the brilliant imagery with which, they are furnished? Or, when involving herself in these novel scenes amidst insurmountable difficulties, and calling lustily for assistance, she awakes Fear from his nod, what enables him to calculate correctly the extent of the ideal danger, and to reason with logical accuracy—only from a false postulate?

I had been indulging in a very delightful dream. The graceful form of S——— was painted in my sleeping fancy, dressed in bridal white, and her fair countenance radiant with smiles. She presented me a letter with a myrtle leaf for the device of the seal, and the words, "*Je ne change qu'en mourant*"—impressed upon the wax. In her other hand was a nosegay of orange flowers; whilst her sister beckoned to me to haste and open the letter, which appeared to have some mysterious connection with my fate. I obeyed, but reluctantly, for I felt a strange dread of the contents. As I proceeded to break the seal, a grim figure, dressed in black, suddenly made his appearance, and in a hollow sepulchral voice, uttered three times the single word, "forbear!" Awed by this solemn warning, I hesitated; but my two friends continuing to encourage me with smiles and gestures, I seized the letter and opened it, notwithstanding the frowns of the gentleman in black. Then, awful sound, a loud clap of thunder awoke me at the instant—not visionary and unreal, but substantial, pealing, atmospheric thunder; accompanied by the most vivid and incessant lightning, and a deluge of rain; which soon dispelled the beautiful illusion, and sent me into the house wet to the skin.

Unfortunately, this hot night, in which I had chosen to sleep, *al fresco*, and to dream all manner of delightful things, was the breaking up of the monsoon, which is always terminated by a terrific storm. The elements continued to roar away without intermission for four or five hours: and the resplendent lightning, as it illuminated the big drops of rain with the brightest prismatic colours, appeared as playful as if it was the most harmless thing in nature.

The change in the aspect of the vegetable world next morning, was most striking—the four months' dust had been washed off the face of the earth—the grass had already begun to shew its tender green —the air was cool, clear and balmy, and the frame felt refreshed as the lungs gulped in the invigorating fluid; and the spirits, long depressed by heat, dust and other discomforts, recovered their elasticity and cheerfulness.

I breakfasted with the M——s, but S—— did not make her appearance. I was concerned at this, as I wanted to give her a laugh at my expense, by relating my adventure of the night before. There appeared a *géné* and singular air about the whole *menage*—especially in the deportment of the host and his wife, much at variance with everything I had before witnessed in that happy and united family. After breakfast M—— requested me to walk into the library, and thus addressed me—"My dear fellow, I perceive there has been a sad mistake. We all esteem you highly, and wish for the continuance of your friendship; but—but—S—— has been for some months engaged to be married to a gentleman in Calcutta."

When one cannot adequately express excited feelings on any subject, it is wise to be silent—a line of conduct sanctioned by great examples, and convenient on the present occasion.

Crabbe's graphic pen has described the different appearance of external nature under opposite moods of mind, in the case of a lover visiting his mistress, and returning from the interview. I cannot approach within a thousand leagues of his inimitable touches, but I can tell in my own homely way, how miserable I felt that day. As I returned, the

air, so deliciously pure in the morning, felt muggy and unrespirable—
the heat was intolerable—the mosquitoes atrociously sanguinary and
numerous—nothing was as it ought, and everything as it ought not to
be. The *palanquin* bearers jerked and shook me, as if on purpose. At my
evening visit to the hospital, several patients were worse, that should
have been better, and had evidently retrograded intentionally, as if to
spite me. At dinner the *punkahs* did not move properly—the mulligatawny was cold, and the wine hot; even Bhastee Rhamm, the *non-
pareil* of *hookabadars*, failed to please. At last I went to bed, thoroughly
disgusted—but even there misfortune continued its persecutions; for
two or three vagrant mosquitoes had slipped in when the servant was
closing the gauze around me, and it was *slap—slap—slap—buzz, buzz,
buzz,* all night.

CHAPTER 27

Voyage from Dinapore to Cawnpore

Ganges, who seemed asleep to lie,
Beheld them with averted eye.

Southey.

In June 1816, the regiment received orders to prepare for a move to Cawnpore, and in the beginning of July, we embarked on the Ganges, now full to the brim.

If any person wishes to luxuriate amongst roses, let him repair to Ghazepore, where the whole country, for some hundred or two of square miles, is thickly covered with them. Rose water and the exquisite Attar of roses are, consequently, cheaper here than in any other part of India; though the latter, when genuine, must always be a most expensive article, from the enormous consumption of roses in its preparation. It takes a prodigious quantity of the petals to make an ounce of *Attar*, and to produce a quart bottle, would require, I suppose, a heap about as big as St. Paul's.

We reached the far-famed Benares on the 8th of July, and anchored at the opposite side of the river. This is a large and very populous city, containing, it is said, some half a million of inhabitants. The streets are extremely narrow—.in fact, nothing more than lanes, about six feet broad, generally. The Brahminee bulls appeared to lead the happiest lives of any creature in this holy city; roaming through the streets as they pleased,—gentle, and sleek, and fat—the domestic gods of the Hindoos. We observed them poking their noses into every confectioner's shop they passed, and always getting a handful of sweets, which they licked up nicely. We saw three disgusting naked *fakeers* perambulating the town, attended by a train of devotees and followers—many of whom were women—these fellows would be famous subjects for the tread-mill.

One of these extraordinary ascetics resided in a hut not far from the place where our Fleet *lagowed*. I went to visit him, and found him a miserable object, scarcely human in appearance, lying on a bed of sharp spikes, with one hand closed, which he had vowed ten or twelve years before, *never* to open. Consequently the nails had pierced through the hand, and stuck out of the back of it, eight or nine inches long; curved, crooked, and sharp, and altogether the most frightful talons imaginable. When I entered the hut I questioned him as to the nature of the crime that had required such terrible expiation—but he made no answer, and when I repeated the question, he scowled forbiddingly and continued silent. I left him gazing listlessly on the Ganges, of which his bed of torture commanded a good view.

The Mosque of Aurungzebe, with its lofty and delicate minarets, is one of the most pleasing and prominent objects in Benares; but its history is disgraceful to its tyrannical and cruel founder. The view from the top is one of the finest in India. The *ghauts*, or steps leading to the river, are remarkable for their vastness and solidity, to say nothing of their usefulness—the Shewallah Ghaut is particularly superb. They are always covered with immense crowds of people going to or returning from their devotions and ablutions—whilst the finely shaped and graceful Hindoo females, bearing their *vasiform* pitchers of water on their heads, thread the mazes of this moving mass of life with great dexterity, and give a classic air to the whole scene.

As on my former voyage up the Ganges, whenever we mounted the stream slowly, I explored the marshes and jungles with my gun, and had good sport amongst the snipe, partridges, and water fowl—the latter were very abundant.

But there is one sad drawback on the pleasure of voyaging on this noble stream—there is one disgusting spectacle which is constantly meeting the eye—human corpses, made buoyant by decomposition, floating down the river; with the odious vultures tearing and disembowelling them as they slowly pass your boat! I know nothing more painful than this sad and humiliating sight. When we consider that the valley of the Ganges contains about thirty millions of souls, and that the dead are for the most part committed to the sacred river; taking also into consideration the great heat of the climate, we may form some opinion of the immense number of bodies that come to the surface, and the enormous mass of putrefaction that is borne on the face, and imbedded in the depths of the stream.

Is it wonderful that Cholera and other pestilential diseases should abound in this beautiful but foul region; and is it not impossible to shut our eyes to this plain proof of the idolatrous adoration of their river reacting with retributive punishment on the besotted natives? The Goddess Ganesa, under the awful authority of the true *Deity*, outraged by Hindoo crime, casts upon her shores the bodies superstitiously committed to her keeping, charged with pestilence and death. This abominable custom ought, and must be forbidden; and the glorious Ganges must no longer be desecrated by millions of dead bodies, and cease to be the great sewer of the accumulated putridity of Bengal.

But these weighty considerations, however natural to a reflecting spectator, are a little too grave for my book. It is more consonant with its light and unpretending character, to relate the numerous instances in which I avenged insulted humanity, by destroying those odious birds, when employed at their horrid feast. I had three barrels always charged with large shot, and never failed to punish them, when possible. I made open war, also, on the alligators: but their mail was not so easily pierced, and they were only vulnerable about the eyes. But the young reptiles were not so protected, and I often shot them lying asleep beside the dam, on the small sandy islets of the river.

Our commanding officer, on this voyage, was an extremely ignorant man, a constant source of amusement from the malapropisms he sported on all occasions. When he heard a new word, especially a long one, he was sure to repeat it, mutilated of some of its fair proportions. During one severe thunderstorm, I happened to observe that the lightning was particularly vivid—next day this was *flivid*—the electric bolt became a *boulder*, and the common military word, defaulter, was murdered, in common with vocables of greater sound, and turned into *defunct*. "Pray Colonel," enquired Lady Lowe, at St. Helena, "how do you manage to have so nice a garden at Francis Plain? Do you employ any of the Chinese labourers?"

"No," was the answer, "we employ nobody but our defuncts."

"Indeed, Colonel—well, that *is* extraordinary. But, I believe it is very judicious, as *they* ought to know something of the soil."

This gentleman often asked me to his *budgerow* during the voyage. There were a couple of unmarried sisters on board, near relations of the family; and when we anchored at some pleasant spot on the bank, it was customary for the colonel, the young ladies and myself, to explore the neighbourhood in the cool of the evening.

One calm and clear evening, when the fleet had *lagowed* for the night at a rich mango *tope*, with smooth velvet turf underfoot, the sisters, the colonel and myself, strolled along the beautiful bank—the elder on his arm and the younger on mine. The pairs, however, soon separated, and my companion and I sauntered along, following a path through the trees, until sunset: we then discovered that we were two miles from the boats, and the short twilight of the East soon began to darken apace. Hastening home, we left the circuitous path we had come by and tried a near-cut through a field; but here an unforeseen obstacle interposed. A rivulet, which, higher up we had crossed by a rustic bridge of a log thrown over it, had become wider and deeper as it approached the Ganges, and now required a good running leap.

In this dilemma I proposed to go round by the bridge, but my young friend would not hear of it—"You have no idea how active I am—jump first and I'll bet you a pair of gloves I'll follow." Then, after another remonstrance, and the expression of a hope, as delicately as such an idea could be embodied in words, that her undergarments were sufficiently capacious—I jumped over. Angela then took a running leap, following the leader; but, alas! the petticoats of those days were very circumscribed—the envious muslin clung around, and hampered the active limbs of the unfortunate young lady; who, arrested in mid career, uttered a piercing shriek and plumped into the middle of the torrent.

At first I could not help a slight laugh, but I soon perceived it was no laughing matter, as the stream was six or seven feet deep and running with great rapidity, and I knew not well what to do. Throwing myself in, however gallant and chivalrous, would be useless, as I should also be borne away by the strong current. So, telling Angela there was no danger, I ran down the bank, parallel with the floating and screaming Beauty, and waiting for a favourable opportunity to make a snatch. After one or two failures I caught her bonnet, but the riband under the chin gave way, and down the torrent she went, with her loosened hair streaming behind her on the water like a mermaid's. At last, when she had been carried down a hundred yards, I succeeded in seizing a handful of her humid tresses, and brought her safe to land.

Poor lady, she was sadly frightened; and as she clung to me more affectionately than was quite comfortable, considering the state of her clothes, I heard such honied expressions, as "guardian angel," "preserver of my life," "debt of everlasting gratitude," uttered, *sotto voce*; which, however, I was not bound to hear. She deferred the hysterics until we reached the boat, but then we had them in abundance.

Allahabad, a fortified town, at the junction of the Jumna and the Ganges, is a very sacred place with the Hindoos, as most points of confluence of the river tributaries are. When we passed, we saw some thousands of the natives, busy in their penitentiary and sacrificial ablutions; which, the Brahmins teach, not only atone for past sin, but purchase uninterrupted ages of happiness.

Suttees, or the voluntary immolation of widows by fire, together with the corpses of their husbands, were not of uncommon occurrence at this time in India. I witnessed one during the voyage on the opposite side of the river, and not far from Allahabad.

This cruel scene took place close to the water's edge, near a huge Banyan tree, whose branches, spreading far and wide, were supported by the vigorous shoots they had sent down into the earth—now grown into strong pillars—like decrepit parents by the piety of their children. It was about ten o'clock at night, and, I suppose, two hundred people were present. The victim was very young—not more than seventeen or eighteen—and though looking a little wild, yet she distributed the flowers and sweetmeats to her friends and relations, with a certain degree of composure; and then mounted the pyre with a firm step, kissed her husband's lips and lay down beside him.

Before this time several fruitless attempts had been made by two of my brother-officers and myself to dissuade her from this terrible self-sacrifice—No, no—if she lived she would be an outcast from society—forced to perform the lowest offices—lose her high *caste* (she was a Brahmin) and be contemned and despised henceforward, by all her acquaintances, friends and relatives. Thus artfully have the Hindoo priests intertwined their sanguinary rites with human pride and vanity, and made these cogent principles subservient to their own ambitious and avaricious purposes.

As soon as this unfortunate woman had placed herself beside her husband, a kind of cage made of bamboos was put over them, smeared with *ghee*, or buffalo-butter, to make it more combustible, and a horrible din of *tom toms*, gongs and human voices was set up; evidently for the purpose of stifling the poor creature's cries. A quantity of dry wood, leaves, &c., surrounded the funeral pile, and was now set fire to, and blazed up fiercely at once, so as, in all probability to save farther suffering, and suffocate the victim in a few seconds. In a short time the whole was one glowing flame, which, when swayed to one side by the wind, gave the spectators a glimpse of the two blackened objects in the centre. The most abominable apathy pervaded the crowd—scarcely a muscle in any face moved; and when the middle of the bodies was consumed, the woman's own relations pushed the bones of the two skulls and the legs into the fiercest part of the fire with long bamboo poles. It was altogether a dreadful sight—an infernal sacrifice, at the perpetration of which demons might rejoice!

Yet, there were not wanting wise men who dreaded danger to the stability of our Indian Empire, from putting an end at once to this hideous custom; but, scarcely a whisper has been heard in opposition to the mandate of Lord William Bentinck, abolishing' the practice for ever. Thus, also, with respect to the custom of committing dead bodies to the Ganges—so loathsome and so pestilential—it only requires a similar edict to rescue that noble stream from pollution.

When we witness all these horrors in Heathen lands, it is scarcely possible for the most thoughtless to avoid reflecting on the infinite obligations our favoured quarter of the globe is under to Christianity, and society generally, in all places pervaded by its influence. Christian women, too, have been placed under a vast debt of gratitude to this benign Religion. Its divine Founder raised them to an equality with the other sex, by his countenance and gracious society when he lived on earth, and by the ennobling influence of his doctrines ever since, and the tone of purity which they have shed over human relations.

Fresh triumphs of Christianity in favour of the weaker, but more virtuous sex, are now passing daily before our eyes; amongst which the recent abolition of female infanticide and widow-burnings in the East, stand out in strong relief. In the Polynesian Archipelago, we also witness the progressive instruction, purification, and elevation of the female savage in the social scale—or rather we see the elements of society created, where all was dark, dismal, and bloody barbarism before.

And well, and zealously, and affectionately, has woman paid her tribute of good works for the benefits her sex has received from Christianity, from the very times of its first promulgation, till the present day. Indeed its propagation, under a superintending Providence, was much dependant on the ministry of women, and their powerful suasion with the rougher half of mankind; and amidst multiplied instances of early bad conduct and apostasy amongst men—there is only one solitary case of female guilt amongst the Apostolic converts; and she, Sapphira, acted plainly under the evil influence of her husband. No woman ever slighted, or neglected, or despised, or blasphemed, or betrayed the

Author of Christianity, or any of his Apostles—No—no.

She ne'er with treacherous kiss her Saviour stung—
Nor e'er denied him with unholy tongue:
She, when Apostles shrank, could danger brave—
Last at his Cross, and earliest at his grave!

CHAPTER 28

Cawnpore

Helleborum frustra, cum jam cutis aegra tumebit,
Poscentes videas; venienti occurrite morbo.

Persius

On the 7th of August, we came in sight of Cawnpore, a pictur-esque military Cantonment, extending five miles along a fine high bank of the Ganges. No barracks being vacant for our reception, we were most unwisely left in our boats, at the opposite side of the river, in a low, marshy neighbourhood, about three weeks. The Ganges hav-ing some time before attained its highest elevation, the waters were now subsiding rapidly, and large tracts were exposed to a powerful sun, that were covered with animal and vegetable pestilence. This was rep-resented at the time, and encamping the regiment on a dry plain near the cantonment, was recommended, but in vain. The consequence was—it may be fairly averred—a fatal Remittent Fever broke out, which in four months carried off five officers and 150 men.

During this time, the duties of the medical officers were no sine-cure. Each of us had charge of a large hospital, and there was one be-sides for sick women; which, I may observe in passing, was altogether supported by the munificence of our worthy commanding officer, Colonel Nicol. We generally had upwards of two hundred cases of fever daily, and one week, close on three hundred. As the weather became cooler in October, the violence of the disease subsided a lit-tle, but it did not cease altogether till January; and then the soldiers were merely the shadows of what they had been: every man, except about half a dozen, having had an attack of fever, and some, two or three times over. It was very melancholy and painful, to see the state to which those noble fellows were reduced by mismanagement, who had so recently mustered nine hundred strong, and in the most glowing vigour of health, on the heights of Muckawnpore.

In these desultory pages it would be out of character to enter into professional details. I shall confine myself to the observation, that as we found in Bengal a strong prejudice running against Dr. Sangrado and his system of depletion, we at first hesitated as to general bleeding to any extent, in our fever cases. Finding, however, that the men died fast, when treated on the authorized system, we abandoned it—prescribed for our patients as we would in Europe, and with striking benefit for the change. Formerly we had lost some twenty-five *per cent*— now five or six was the amount.

Most of our officers occupied comfortable Bungalows, with, gardens, at Cawnpore—I lived in a good house, with a large garden, and kept a gardener and a couple of oxen. The chief business of the latter was to eat, and chew the cud, and, as an amusement, to put their shoulders to the wheel for half an hour a-day, to raise water for irrigating the garden. On my first arrival I found several illegal occupiers of my premises—namely, a large colony of muskrats, who had built a subterranean city in one of my best beds. These little wretches used to come out of their burrows at night, to make predatory incursions into the house, eating and carrying off what they could, and defiling by their odious and indelible taint, everything they touched. Incredible as it may appear, it is a fact, that this strong odour is communicated to wine or brandy in sealed bottles, by these creatures merely passing over them—I had a couple of dozen of brandy spoiled thus at Cawnpore: the *modus operandi* I never could make out.

My patience being at last worn out by multiplied nuisances committed by these unsavoury animals—of which the corrupting my Cognac was the climax—I determined to exterminate the whole race. Accordingly I sent to the barracks, and collected all the curs that could be found in the precincts—amounting to three or four dozen. After five or six preliminary fights amongst this heterogeneous pack, and a due administration of the whip, to put them in some decent order, we proceeded to the hunt.

First—two *bheesties*, or water-carriers, with their pig-skins full of water, were ordered to beat the coverts. Inserting: the muzzle of a pipe, attached to the forefoot of the pig's hide, in one of the central holes of the principal burrow, the *bheestie* played away vigorously until he had emptied his skin, when he was relieved by the other; and as the garden well was near, and the bullocks hard at work, water was abundant, and the stream ran uninterruptedly into the subterranean caves of the rats. The tenacious little animals stood the inundation with great courage, which to them must have been nearly as formidable as the Thames bursting into the Tunnel amongst Mr. Brunei's workmen. At last, when the water spread far and wide, and there was no possibility of remaining any longer, they crept out of their holes half drowned, and were all destroyed by the dogs.

There were two or three fine *Peepuhl* trees in the garden, which were objects of my special admiration. When I awoke one morning, soon after taking possession, I heard the most horrid noise and screaming close to my window; and on questioning the *sirdar* bearer, who always slept at the threshold, he said it was only the parrots, and he would soon drive them away. Next morning it was repeated; when I started up and saw about a thousand paroquets—active rascals, with red beaks, rich green plumage, and long tails—demolishing the buds and blossoms, and eating and screaming with all their might. The trees were actually loaded with them, and the branches bent down almost to the ground. Notwithstanding my bearer's repugnance to destroy animal life, I made him bring my gun, and sent the contents of two barrels amongst the marauders, which killed fifty or sixty of them. I know not whether this noisy tribe have ever been deemed of any value, except in the oratorical department. Feeling several of those I shot plump and fat, I directed them to be cooked for breakfast, and my Curry turned out a very good dish.

I presume that everybody has heard of the feats of Indian Jugglers, and many persons have seen a celebrated magician in London, named Raamoh Saame, whose beautiful performance with the brass balls before the glass-curtain of the Coburgh Theatre was much admired. In 1822, I saw him keep *nine* of these balls in motion at the same time; which is, I believe, the *ne plus ultra* as to numbers, and a striking spectacle it was—for the duplication of the bright little globes in the gigantic mirror, enhanced much the grace and effect of the performance. When our detachment was quartered at Poonamalee on our first arrival from England, a far-famed Madras Juggler paid us a visit to astonish the Griffins, as they called us Johnny New- comes, and put a few *rupees* into the girdle of his long robe. This clever fellow began by swallowing a sword, the point of which I felt in his stomach—ate fire—turned cards into chickens, and chickens into full-grown cocks; and sent eight balls on their travels round his body—moving simultaneously and harmoniously in their different orbits—infallible as the planets—with many other astonishing things.

As the soldiers were staring at him, he caught the eye of one man, in whose countenance there was an air of peculiar surprise. He addressed him immediately in English—"I make you lay one egg here," putting his hand on the soldier's forehead. The man stared and blushed, but at length exclaimed with a shake of the head, "I'se d—— if you can, though."

The officers being desirous to find out how this trick was done, both juggler and soldier were stripped naked, and brought into an empty room in which there was full light from a strong sun. The magician then made the man sit down on the floor in the middle of the room; and an ingenuous Yorkshire lad he was, who looked up at the yellow juggler with a good-natured grin and strong expression of incredulity. The performer then proceeded to fix his eye, and to walk round him slowly and deliberately seven times, repeating some unintelligible gibberish. He then quickened his pace for seven more gyrations—and still increased it for seven additional circles, fascinating his eye, gesticulating and uttering strange sounds as before. At the end of the third series he slapped the man on the forehead with the open palm—when, lo! out started a fine fresh egg! The soldier was so astonished that he ran out of the room, naked as he was, swearing that the juggler was the devil.

Now, although five of us watched the whole proceeding with minute attention, in a full light; and were, besides, sharpened in our observation by the idea of some trickery, none could discover where or how the egg was concealed. That it was genuine there could be no doubt—for we boiled it, and I ate some of it myself, but the frightened fellow who laid it would not taste it.

One morning at Cawnpore, a native asked permission to speak to *Saahib*. He was admitted, and after a profusion of the most reverential *salaams*, he told me that from certain indications he was sure there were snakes in *Saahib's* garden, which he would engage to catch for half a *rupee* a-piece, being a professed snake-charmer. I closed with his offer immediately, and he said he would come the next morning.

Punctual to his appointment he made his appearance, armed with a long pipe, on which he began to play violently, using various grotesque gesticulations, all over the garden. After keeping up this solo for a quarter of an hour, he stopped suddenly before a low bush near an old tree; played two or three bars, *fortissimo*, and then, plunging his hand into the bush, pulled out a large Cobra de Capello, or hooded snake, and put it into a basket slung to his neck. He proceeded in this way for some time, exploring different parts of the garden; and ended by catching two more snakes. Then, after a little more music, the charmer said there were no more in the garden, and claimed the stipulated reward.

This, I promised to pay him immediately, if he permitted me to destroy the reptiles, which I knew very well he would not allow. I then examined them, and after some trouble, ascertained that two teeth had been pulled from the jaws of each—no doubt the poison fangs—and the animals, in all probability, had been placed in the very spot where they were found the same morning, by collusion of some of the servants. The magician and his basket were then very unceremoniously expelled—the servants abusing him in the choicest Hindustanee Billingsgate, for attempting to impose on wise *Saahib*, who was more learned and sagacious than Suleyman—although some of those very rascals had no doubt entered into the conspiracy against *Saahib's* sagacity.

I met Cobras on several occasions when out shooting, and twice escaped being bit narrowly enough. They are fond of burrowing in a loose sandy soil—particularly about the roots of shrubs and bushes, because, I suppose, they find the diverging roots and radicles convenient, as so many rafters to support the roofs of their houses. One day, when intent on some partridges, I stepped over a Palma Christi plant, and placed my foot almost on the head of a large Cobra just come out of his hole. This trespass he naturally enough resented by erecting his hood, coiling himself up, looking fierce, and preparing for a spring. But, poor fellow, notwithstanding the protection of his own tribe as the symbol of my profession, and the *aegis*, the medicinal plant that overshaded his domicile afforded, I was obliged, in self-defence, to shoot him. He was large of his kind—being seven feet long.

The snake-charmers in India, who make these creatures dance to music, effect their object, I believe, in a way, and from motives on the part of the snake, that are imperfectly understood. Notwithstanding popular belief, as old as the time of Alexander the Great, and deemed worthy of notice amongst the wonders of India, by Arrian the Historian, I suspect that snakes have no "music in their soul," and are not to be charmed—notwithstanding appearances to the contrary—by " concord of sweet sounds." On a careful analysis, I fear the poetry of the matter is reducible to very unromantic and simple elements. The snake, previously deprived of its death-fangs, is kept coiled up in a basket with two or three others, equally harmless; and when one is wanted for an exhibition, the juggler seizes him by the neck, hauls him out of the basket and throws him rudely on the ground. This raises the reptile's choler—which, I fancy, is not a difficult matter—it hisses, bristles out its hood and erects its head.

The charmer, playing away on his noisy pipe, confronts the enraged creature, as if about to tread on it; but adroitly moves about beyond the reach of its spring. Thus fixing and fascinating the animal's eye, he keeps describing a half-circle—perpetually in motion, menacing the snake, and obliging it to move as he moves—in momentary expectation that he will approach within its reach, and prepared to dart on him, if he does—which never happens. This quick oscillation of the creature in pure anger and self-defence—perhaps in disgust at the barbarous music—is attributed by the spectators to its fondness for the very sounds it cordially hates—people go away delighted with the effect of the magician's pipe—all manner of quotations relating to the power of music are made; and, perhaps, some fond parent goes home idolizing the science, and resolved to get the best masters for his leaden-eared daughter, Clementina, who will never distinguish one note from another.

Cawnpore is supposed by some antiquarians to have been the site of Palibothra, of the era of Alexander the Great. In more modern times the immense city of Kanouge stood on the bank, part of which is now occupied by British barracks. This place is said to have contained twenty thousand Betel shops alone—yet one *pagoda* is now the solitary vestige of so vast a city. There is an extensive Mohammedan burying-ground in the neighbourhood, containing many fine tombs, and much frequented, like all Moslem cemeteries, by the relations of the deceased. But, in this climate which rusts and ruins everything, except the scythe of time—the most magnificent and solid buildings soon fall to decay.

CHAPTER 29

Route for St. Helena

O magic of love! unembellished by you
Has the garden a blush, or the herbage a hue?
Or blooms there a prospect in nature or art
Like the vista that shines through the eye to the heart?

Moore.

In the beginning of January 1817, we received the unexpected and unwelcome intelligence that our regiment was soon to proceed to Calcutta, and embark for St. Helena, where Napoleon was detained a prisoner of war by the English Government. As at this time arrangements were making for a grand campaign against the Phindarrie hordes, and stirring times were approaching, we were not at all pleased with the prospect of leaving the country. Besides, the idea of changing our luxurious Indian living for the mackerel and yams of that barren Islet, was by no means agreeable, to say nothing of the state of constraint and vigilance to which we should be subject; but there was no remedy.

Our relations of mutual friendship had not been broken off by the vanishing of any prospect of nearer connexion; and my friend M—— and myself had corresponded regularly since the regiment left Dinapore. He now resided in Allahabad, and was commandant of that fortress. As soon as he learned that we were coming down the river, he sent me a warm invitation to stay a week or ten days with him in passing, which I accepted, and started on a fortnight's leave to Allahabad.

I found this amiable family well; and was not a little surprised to meet S—— still unmarried. She was in distress; for some unfavourable disclosures had been made respecting the character of her lover, and his honour was suspected relative to certain gambling transactions, in which he had been engaged at Calcutta. Besides all this, he had been dangerously ill; and was now cruising about in a pilot schooner off the Sunderbunds, by medical advice. I was received with the most affectionate cordiality by every member of the family.

Lovely affianced girls should not be permitted to move about in society for any considerable time, breaking people's hearts hopelessly, and spreading distress and envy, and all kinds of bad feelings and sensations around. They ought to be made to marry within the month by act of Parliament. Here, for instance, was myself brought once more within the circle of a very delightful young lady's charms; and under circumstances, too, that did not altogether preclude hope. Yet, though well aware of the danger of my position, I had neither the power nor wish to fly from the dangerous fascination. Even the confiding freedom of her manner—reposing trust in my sense of propriety; and the easy unreserve of our intercourse, whilst they shewed the unaffected ingenuousness of her nature, excited distressing repinings at perceiving the full value of the prize allotted to another.

Thus delicately circumstanced, I spent a fortnight at Allahabad—a golden time. The whole family, from some over-estimate they had formed of certain professional services I had done one of them, considered themselves under obligations, when in truth, I was the obliged party. They therefore, one and all, exerted themselves to crowd into this final visit, before we should part for a long separation, every *agrément* and pleasure possible—morning and evening drives on beautiful roads—dinners, dances, music, Waverley Novels—then in full blow, and brought from Calcutta by *dawk*, or post. In short, whatever of agreeableness and enjoyment the kindest solicitude of refined minds could suggest, and ample means afford, were concentrated in that exquisite visit.

I told them of the Suttee I had witnessed in the neighbourhood, and learned that three more of these horrid sacrifices had occurred near the town lately. In fact, human life seemed of small value there; for instances of voluntary drowning, as an atonement for sin, were common enough—particularly at the precise point of junction of the rivers, which was eminently sacred. Old bedridden people were constantly brought to the shore of the Ganges, their mouths were stuffed with the river-mud, and there they were left to perish. At one of the Suttees the ladies had fruitlessly endeavoured to prevent the widow from submitting to the dreadful decree of selfish and sanguinary Brahmins, of whose income these sacrifices used to form a large part.

In the course of my intercourse with the major, I saw and learned a good deal of the character of the Indian *sepoy*, but chiefly of the native soldier of Bengal. It is altogether, a fine one. The Bengal *sepoy* is distinguished for temperance, docility, fidelity to his officers, and a large share of courage. The corps which my friend commanded had fought most bravely at the storm of Bhurtpore, and vied with the King's regiments in their desperate attempts to overcome insurmountable obstacles on that fatal occasion. He and two of his grenadiers had succeeded, after a murderous struggle, in reaching nearly the top of the Breach, when one of the brave fellows was shot, and the major was knocked down by a stone dropped on his head, and rolled to the bottom. There he lay insensible, and must have been soon despatched, but for the other grenadier, who watched over him, and bore him out of the ditch in his arms—receiving a severe wound from a matchlock ball, as he carried him off. This noble fellow was, most deservedly, made a *havildar* on his recovery; and, following up this good conduct, had been recently promoted to the rank of *jemidar*—equivalent to our lieutenant. He was pointed out to me when I was at Allahabad, and I never saw a finer looking man. My gallant friend assured me that he felt as certain of the attachment and devotion of his regiment as of his own family.

In corps like his, whose recruiting had been carefully conducted, and into which low-*caste* Hindoos, and Mussulmans were refused admittance, there exists a high sense of honour, or *esprit de corps*. Nor do the high-*caste* Moslems and Hindoos quarrel in the same regiments; for it is a point of importance to mix them: but they conduct themselves much the same as Protestants and Catholics in the British Army. They have separate messes, and respect each other's particular customs; and thus, very generally go on harmoniously together under the salutary restraint of strict discipline; confiding implicitly in their officers and in the Company's Government.

The day before my departure, my friend drove me to see an enormous *Banyan* tree in the neighbourhood, that covered between two and three acres of ground. The age nobody could tell ; but it was supposed to be a thousand years old. Very probably it was underrated; for when a healthy Antaeus of the vegetable world like this, is once set a going, as long as there is soil and surface enough, I can see no limits to its progress—on it goes, multiplying its own existence, but not perishing after conferring life; still throwing out its grotesque horizontal arms through a long succession of ages, and deriving support and fresh nourishment from the thousand columnar props and suckers that connect them with the earth.

A great change had taken place in the river since we last sailed on it—the water had fallen about thirty feet; and large tracts over which we had passed, were now covered with luxuriant crops of rice and other grain. The high banks along which we coasted when the wind was contrary, being composed of loose alluvial materials, used to come tumbling about our ears rather alarmingly—often threatening to swamp our boat.

At Benares, I paid a visit to the *fakir* of the spiky hand. There he was, exactly as before—in the same attitude—wrapped in pride, sulky and silent, and gazing on the sun and the river, I spoke to him in his own language, but he would not condescend to answer.

At Dinapore, on this voyage, the career of my eccentric friend, L——t, was closed. Being apprehensive of meeting his creditors at Calcutta, he desired his servant, the evening of our arrival, to put a bottle of brandy on the table and leave the cabin of the boat. He then commenced drinking and smoking, and singing German songs; whilst all the other officers were at a ball given by the 24th Regiment. Having finished his brandy he drew his sword, attacked the boatmen and his native servants, then, having cleared the boat, he waved his weapon several times over his head, spouted something to the moon, that was shining at the time, and jumped into the Ganges. The river ran deep and rapid, and his body was never found.

Headquarters of the Regiment, with three hundred men, embarked at Calcutta on the 2nd April 1817, in the ship *Dorah*, for St. Helena. Colonel Nicol, our excellent commanding officer, made everything as agreeable as possible during the voyage.